SOME QUESTIONS THIS BOOK ANSWERS:

- Is a will the only way to transfer property at death?

- Why do wills need to be so long?

- Can I write a simple will myself?

- If I need an attorney to make a will, how much will it cost and what questions will I be asked?

- Do I need a will if all of my assets are owned jointly with my spouse?

- Should I leave everything to my spouse?

- Should I leave something for my children? In fact, how much do I have to leave to my spouse?

- I am told life insurance is free from taxes. If this is so, shouldn't I buy a lot of life insurance?

- Speaking of taxes, I am told living trusts save lots of taxes. How can I find out about this and where do I get one?

- What happens if I leave everything I have to my spouse and my spouse remarries? How can I be sure that my children will get something?

- What happens if both of us are deceased and our children are still too young to take care of things?

- This is my second marriage. I want to take care of my spouse. We want to provide for each other and we both have our own children. When both of us are gone, each of us would like our assets to go to our respective children. How do I handle this?

- What's the Florida homestead exemption?

- How do I provide for medical decisions if I am incapacitated?

- How do I provide for financial management of my assets if I am incapacitated? Or if my spouse is incapacitated?

- Will the doctors and hospitals really honor living wills?

- Can I give money away and—with the tax deductions—actually come out ahead?

- When should I start to draw on my pension plan?

ESTATE

PLANNING

IN

FLORIDA

SECOND EDITION

John T. Berteau
Attorney-at-Law

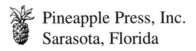

Pineapple Press, Inc.
Sarasota, Florida

121954

To a lady who made this book possible many years ago, my mother, Frances Russo.

Inquires should be addressed to:
Pineapple Press, Inc.
P.O. Box 3899
Sarasota, Florida 34230

This publication is designed to acquaint the reader with general concepts involved in estate planning. It should not be relied upon as a source of legal or tax advice. The reader should seek competent professional counsel before making any estate planning decisions.

All forms and schedules used in this book are provided for educational and illustrative purposes only and are not to be used except on advice of your attorney.

Probate forms in the appendixes are used with the permission of Florida Lawyers Support Services, Inc. The forms are available to attorneys through Florida Lawyers Support Services, Inc., P.O. Box 5647, Tallahassee, Florida 32314, (904) 656-7590.

LIBRARY OF CONGRESS CATALOGING-IN-PUBLICATION
Berteau, John T., 1941–
      Estate planning in Florida / by John T. Berteau—2nd ed.
          p.   cm.
      Includes index.
      ISBN 1-56164-151-0 (alk. paper)
      1. Estate planning—Florida—Popular works.   I. Title.
KFF140.Z9B47   1998
346.75905'2—dc21
98-14520   CIP

Second Edition
10 9 8 7 6 5 4 3 2 1

Cover design by Steve Duckett
Design and composition by Sandra Wright's Designs
Printed and bound by The Maple Press, York, Pennsylvania

CONTENTS

Appendices

ACKNOWLEDGMENTS

In writing a book such as this, there are many persons who offered comments, suggestions, help, and encouragement, but special recognition should be given to Linda Arnold Earle. Her interest and unflagging enthusiasm, together with her experience as a practicing attorney and technical expertise as the holder of an advanced degree in law and taxation, were most helpful. Thanks also to my secretary, Patsy Marcum, who has typed so many drafts and redrafts and has overcome computer glitches. Thanks to Judy Johnson, Patricia Hammond, Sandy Wright, and Kris Rowland for their editorial expertise and to Patricia again for the index. Finally and most importantly, thanks to the thousands of men and women who have sat in my office and discussed estate planning. They taught me much over the years and have brought their life experiences, their learning, and their insights into this book.

INTRODUCTION

Everyone has an estate plan. *No* estate plan is also an estate plan—and it may be a bad one. Seldom is it the plan you would choose for yourself. Each state has enacted a body of laws regulating the transfer of property after the owner's death. If the decedent has a valid will (a testate estate), that will, almost without limitations, directs the transfer, control, and benefit of assets. If there is no valid will (an intestate estate), the generic, one-plan-fits-all "will" designed by the state legislature is imposed.

You might say, "Estate planning is for people with lots of money. I know I need a will, but my neighbors offered to lend me a form kit they ordered. That should be fine for my estate."

You are worth more than you think! Fill out a simple financial sheet similar to the one in Appendix A of this book and total the values. The result may pleasantly surprise you and may suggest that good stewardship is required now to protect the assets you have worked to acquire. And your wealth is only a part of your financial picture. *You* are also an important asset. You provide valuable services for yourself and for others who depend on you. A well-conceived estate plan can help you and them prepare for the time when you are less able or unable to continue these services. Your property and your responsibilities are unique; your estate plan should fit *you*.

You can't take it with you, so estate planning necessarily is concerned with the transfer of wealth at death. But it is rarely so limited in scope or time. An effective plan begins during life (the earlier, the better), is revised as lives and laws change, and may continue to control certain assets long after your death. Estate planning involves far more than simply writing a will or funding a trust. It is more than considering how much the tax gatherer is going to take. It is even more than finding the least expensive way to transfer the greatest amount of property.

Cutting costs is important and may reasonably be your primary objective. Potential savings of money and time justify serious estate planning for almost every size estate. Though a large estate may pay more taxes and other expenses, the smaller costs incurred by a smaller estate often represent a greater percentage of the estate. However, avoiding taxes or probate is not *necessarily* the primary goal of estate planning. Though each of us may experience an occasional twinge of "the-one-who-dies-with-the-most-toys-wins," most people value money mostly for the security and pleasure it provides the people and organizations which are important to them. Good estate planning ultimately considers the effect the plan will have on people, not property. Will the plan truly benefit the intended beneficiaries? Who will be the beneficiaries? When should they receive their benefits? How should they take the property: jointly? in trust? outright? otherwise? Will hard-earned assets be squandered away by a spendthrift? What is the best way to manage your property? Does the family business more appropriately "belong" to one individual? If so, what do you do about it? Could an outright inheritance undermine self-reliance and encourage bad habits, excessive spending, or worse?

Together, you and I and an assortment of clients—both real and imaginary—will explore a practical, money-saving approach to estate planning for the Floridian. We will examine the ways assets can be transferred—with the lowest costs, the smallest amount of red tape, and the fewest delays—to the intended beneficiaries. We will learn ways to save taxes, particularly federal estate taxes, federal income taxes, and state death taxes (Florida does in fact have an estate tax). We will review common planning tools including wills, lifetime gifts, Totten trusts, joint property, life insurance, retirement plans, living wills, living trusts, and durable powers of attorney. We also will look at other, less familiar ideas. We will consider your beneficiaries' needs and your concerns about meeting those needs.

This book is not a "do-it-yourself" or "how-to-avoid-attorneys" primer. Public opinion to the contrary, most attorneys who object to such publications are more concerned about the welfare of the public than about any potential loss of business. Ordinarily, such books change the nature of our practice, not the volume. Instead of being given the relatively easy task of structuring the estate properly up front, we are called in after the fact to provide cleanup or damage control. This book is intended to answer, in plain English, questions which are commonly asked, to pose questions which should be considered, and to make the whole process of planning for the management and preservation of your estate more understandable, less complex, and sufficiently responsive to meet the changing needs of you and your family.

ESTATE

PLANNING

IN

FLORIDA

SECOND EDITION

If you have recently moved to Florida or if you live here for only part of the year, you may want to know:

- Am I a Floridian?
- How do I become a Floridian?
- What is a Declaration of Domicile?
- Do I need a new will?
- How do I find a good attorney?
- What does certification mean?
- Do I need to do anything before the first meeting with my attorney?
- How much will this cost?

1

ARE YOU A FLORIDIAN?

An initial step in the estate planning process is to determine your state of domicile. This is usually easy, unless you have recently moved to Florida or you live here only a portion of the year. The technical term for where you usually live is "domicile." Domicile may not have any obvious connection to your estate plan, so let's see why it is important.

Laws vary among states. In preparing your estate plan, you need to know which rules to follow. If you are a Floridian, you are subject to the laws of Florida. There are limitations on every state's right to impose its laws (its "jurisdiction") on its citizens, just as there are circumstances that give a state jurisdiction over an individual who is not its citizen. While you are driving through Ohio, you must obey Ohio's traffic laws. It does no good to complain "I'm a Floridian and that isn't the law in Florida." If you sell your vacation home in the mountains of North Carolina, the closing will be subject to North Carolina's laws, including payment of fees and taxes imposed by North Carolina. Which brings us to the real issue in many domicile cases: Which state gets to collect how much in taxes?

The differences in the amount of death and inheritance taxes assessed by various states can be significant. Each state in which you live or own property wants a bite of your estate. You—and each state—have a financial interest in locating your domicile.

Florida may not be as well known for its favorable tax climate as for its sunny weather, but both reputations are well deserved. Few states, except perhaps Nevada, are more benevolent in their taxation of estates. Not only are inheritance and death taxes higher in some other states, but also many states, especially those in the Northeast, have become increasingly aggressive in asserting that estate taxes are owed even though the person who died is no longer a resident of the state. This growing trend means there is a need for careful planning in order to reduce exposure to possible conflicting claims against your estate. There is even the remote but real possibility that, without proper planning, you may be legally domiciled in more than one state, and each state will take a full tax bite!

The Intent to Be a Floridian

You are not a Floridian solely because you live here. You must *intend* that Florida be your "usual place of dwelling" (the statutory definition of "domicile" and "residence"). Since "intention" exists solely in a person's mind, it is sometimes difficult to know precisely in which state a person resides. When you additionally consider that different states have different definitions of "domicile" and different standards for asserting jurisdiction over all or some portion of a person's estate, you can understand the potential for conflict and, occasionally, dual citizenship. To avoid the possibility that more than one state might claim jurisdiction over your estate and impose taxes based on such claim, you should clearly establish residence in one state. Visible acts are presumed to indicate your intention; therefore, if you want to be a Floridian, it is important that you act like a Floridian after moving to Florida.

Did You File Your Declaration of Domicile?

The document commonly known as a Declaration of Domicile is a sworn statement that you are currently living in Florida and intend Florida to be your permanent home (or your principal home if you also live part time in another state). The form is in Appendix B in this book or may be obtained from the Clerk of the Circuit Court's office at your local courthouse. Your Declaration of Domicile is filed with that office as part of the public records of your county. You can also write a letter to your former home state, stating that you are now a Floridian and that it should not expect any further taxes from you as a resident of that state.

What else can you do to indicate your intention to be a Floridian? Write a Florida will. Though there are many more important reasons for writing a will than to show your intention to be a Floridian, there are few better ways to show that intention than to execute a will which states that you are a resident of Florida. Register to vote in Florida. Vote. Pay United States income taxes through the Internal Revenue Service office in Atlanta as other Florida citizens do. Open bank accounts in Florida. Transfer your religious, social, and professional organization memberships here. Join and be active in Florida organizations. Spend time in Florida. If you travel a substantial portion of the year or live in several places, stop in your Florida home between moves from one location to another. Pay Florida intangible tax if any is due. Get a Florida driver's license and put a Florida tag on your car. File for your Florida homestead exemption. All these actions indicate that you are a Floridian. Later we'll talk more about some of the problems of having citizenship in two states, but for the time being, the important thing is to be sure you have done everything you can to make yourself a Floridian.

How to Find an Attorney

If you are going to have an attorney help you with your estate plan, your next question may be "How do I pick a good attorney?" An obvious choice is to talk to the attorney who has been doing other legal work for you. If you are not satisfied with your attorney or you do not have one, ask friends or coworkers. The best recommendation is a satisfied client. If none of these sources produces the right name, look in the Yellow Pages. Most attorneys who specialize in estate planning are listed under the subheading "Wills, Trusts, and Estate Planning" or "Estate Planning and Probate— Board Certified" or some similar designation. Don't be misled by large ads.

There can be an inverse relationship between the size of the advertisement and the ability of the attorney. You want high quality, professional legal work at reasonable fees, not extravagant promises and cute graphics.

Certification

The Florida Bar has adopted a system for telling the public which attorneys have special skills in certain areas of the law. Attorneys who have passed a rigorous written exam and peer review and have a satisfactory professional ethics record can apply to the Florida Bar for certification in Estate Planning and Probate for a five-year period. Certification is the highest classification a Florida attorney can attain. While there are many good estate planners who are not certified, you can feel assured that a Bar-certified attorney in estate planning has a good reputation and a proven level of expertise.

How to Prepare for Your First Meeting with Your Attorney

After you have found an attorney and made an appointment, new questions often arise. "What am I supposed to do? What does my attorney do? Should I bring any documents or information? Should I bring my spouse? How much is all of this going to cost?"

If you are meeting with your attorney for the first time, he or she needs to know something about you. You should be able to tell your attorney about yourself, your family, your property, and your planning objectives. Some attorneys have a printed information form which will be sent to you before the first meeting. Others prefer to obtain the necessary information on a person-to-person basis.

If you have an existing will, trust, buy-sell agreement for your business, nuptial agreement, divorce decree, or other similar documents, you could take them, as well as copies of any gift tax returns and recent income tax returns, to your initial meeting. Having this information immediately available will be helpful in the planning process. Though your attorney may not expect you to bring deeds, stock certificates, or life insurance policies for a simple will, all documents of title may need to be reviewed for more complex estate planning.

Legal Fees

Lawyers' fees differ widely and depend on a variety of factors including the complexity of your estate plan, the value and nature of your assets, the possibility of family conflicts or future litigation, the attorney's volume of estate planning practice, the attorney's expertise, and the city in which the attorney practices. However, it is a safe generalization that the cost to have a qualified attorney prepare a simple will is one of the best bargains going. Many attorneys charge less than it costs them to actually prepare the will. They recognize every person's need to have a simple will, and they lower their fees to make this service available to a greater number of people. These attorneys may have additional motives and may provide this service in order to attract new clients or with the hope of handling the estate. Whatever their reasons, you benefit. Take advantage of the opportunity.

In this chapter, you will learn:

- how to make cremation and burial arrangements
- how to handle debts and taxes
- what tangible personal property is
- how to make specific gifts
- the importance of describing real estate
- what "rest, residue and remainder" means
- what a personal representative is
- what powers a personal representative should have
- how to handle real estate outside Florida
- the advantages of a self-proving affidavit
- how to make your will and store it safely

2

THE SIMPLE WILL—KEPT SIMPLE

Before meeting with your attorney to discuss your will, you may want to consider what your will should (and shouldn't) say about the subjects listed above. We will discuss making your will and safekeeping your executed will in this chapter.

The best known, most used, and least complex estate planning device is the simple will. A will is a written statement of an individual's directions for the transfer of his or her property which is to take effect after his or her death. In order for the document to be effective as a valid will (admitted to probate), it must be signed as required by law. These laws haven't changed much during the past several centuries, regardless of your state of domicile, so it is important to take advantage of a relatively modern innovation, the self-proving affidavit. But, let's write your will first.

Everyone who has assets should have a will, whether or not those assets have significant value. Remember, the State of Florida has, in effect, written a will for every Floridian who dies without a valid will. As occasionally happens when the government steps in, the procedure becomes more time-consuming and more expensive, and it may not produce a result anyone likes. A simple will is the way to avoid this problem.

Printed will forms are available at stationery stores, through television and newspaper advertisements, and via computer software. These forms generally result in a very poor will. A document intended to be used by a large segment of the public addresses only those matters most common to all, in the manner most suitable for all. The individual all too frequently has to conform to the form.

The best choice is to have a reputable attorney prepare a will for you. Attorneys use a variety of form wills also, but your attorney begins with a basic form which is right for you and then revises that form to do what you want it to do. More importantly, you will have the opportunity to ask and to be asked questions you need to consider. Remember, everything you own will be tied up in this document. Mistakes and omissions discovered after the will takes effect can't be corrected.

A simple will just looks simple. Numerous options and alternatives can, and often should, be considered during the drafting process. Initially, you should realize that the designation "simple will" is not a legal term, though it is generally understood to mean a will that leaves everything directly to specified beneficiaries. No trusts, special tax provisions, or complex formulas for dividing the estate are included in a simple will. Typically, a simple will might leave everything to the spouse, if surviving, and, if not, equally to the children. What should the simple will—or for that matter any will—say? What should be omitted?

Introductory Clause

The initial paragraph is ordinarily a single sentence: "I, John Smith, a resident of Tangerine County, Florida, declare this to be my Last Will and Testament and revoke all prior wills and codicils." (Codicil is the legal term for an amendment to your will.)

If you are commonly known by a name other than or in addition to your legal name, you should include both names, for example, "Barbara Eaton

Thorton Howard, also known as Beth Howard."

Naming Florida as your place of residence is considered an indication of your intent to be a Floridian and helps establish domicile. This statement also helps determine the county in which your estate will be probated.

On the other hand, your assurance that you are "of sound mind and body" does not prove anything and is generally omitted. You must be of sound mind and at least eighteen years old to have the "testamentary capacity" which entitles you to make a will in Florida, but this traditional affirmation has been discarded along with "heretofore," "aforesaid," and other legalese as excess verbiage. If your competency at the time you execute your will could become an issue because of advancing age, illness, undue influence, duress, or any other reason, more aggressive and effective measures are necessary. Under such circumstances, it would be advisable to obtain written statements from friends or your doctor, an expert opinion regarding your testamentary capacity, or medical records to document the reasons you chose to dispose of your assets in a particular way or to prepare any other records which appropriately address the potential issue. These records should be compiled and executed at the time your will is written but not included in the actual will.

Neither praise nor recrimination belongs in a will. Words of appreciation are best shared during life. Moreover, an intended gift to "Mary Brown, my devoted secretary whom I could never adequately repay for all her invaluable assistance to me over the years" may be treated as additional compensation to Mary. Unnecessary facts and personal opinions rarely serve any valid purpose. Not naming a family member as a beneficiary has the effect of disinheriting that person. If you want to clarify your intention, it is sufficient to say, "I make no provision for my oldest daughter, Barbara Ann." Barbara Ann may be a multimillionaire, a drug addict, or an adult child from whom you are presently estranged. Feelings and circumstances change, so don't explain, at least not in your will. When you die, your will becomes part of the public records in your county. If you want to have the last word or to set the record straight, you may subject your estate to a lawsuit.

A new will generally revokes all prior wills and codicils, but it is best to be very clear about your intention.

Cremation and Burial

Instructions for your funeral and burial generally do not belong in your will. After all, the will may not be read until after the service. If the arrangements were not in accordance with your wishes, remorse, guilt, or bitterness may result. There is one exception. A statement of your intention to be cremated is helpful, particularly in those situations where there is no close family member or there are family members who disagree on this issue. If the person in charge of your estate (named the "personal representative" in Florida, "executor" in some other states) arranges for cremation according to the instructions in your will or in a written contract which you signed, that person is protected if sued for allowing the cremation. A simple, direct sentence—"I desire that my body be cremated"—is sufficient.

Whatever your preference may be, talk with your clergy, family, or close friends so the appropriate persons are aware of your choice. Leave the specifics in a letter with these individuals, or make arrangements with a funeral home.

Debts and Taxes

Many wills contain some instructions concerning payment of "my just debts" and taxes. Generally, it is best to omit any reference to your debts and to let your attorney worry about the technicalities of apportioning taxes (identifying who should pay how much of what tax). A saying survives from old English law to the effect that one must be just before one can be generous. Rest assured, valid creditors will file their claims and be paid. Specific instruction should be included in your will if you want your personal representative to pay any charitable pledge or other moral obligation which you are not legally obligated to repay, or to pay off an existing mortgage before encumbered property is transferred to the designated beneficiary.

Tangible Personal Property

Next, generally, comes a section distributing the tangible personal property. Tangible personal property is a legal term and is much preferred to general, vague terms such as personal effects. There are three general categories of property: real property (real estate), intangible personal property (stocks, bonds, partnership interests, money, promissory notes, and other pieces of paper or similar items which are not valuable in and of themselves, but which represent a promise of or an interest in something which is valuable), and tangible personal property (everything else). The last category includes things such as pots and pans, jewelry, furniture, boats, airplanes, paintings, tools, shotguns, silver and crystal, rare coins—all the things you own personally, even if you use them in your business. Give some thought to these items. This is one of the areas where the most problems occur. There is a saying among estate planners that people get angry over the tangible personal property, then fight over the money.

There are four common ways to give away tangible personal property. Each has its pros and cons so ordinarily a combination of methods is used. Think about which would be best for you and talk to your attorney.

The General Statement

The general statement has no detailed enumeration of the tangible personal property, so it is the simplest and frequently the best way to give away ("devise" or "bequeath") this property. Beth's will could provide: "I give all my tangible personal property to William, my husband, and if my husband is deceased, then equally to my children, Elizabeth, Robert, and Blake, as shall survive me to be divided among them as they may agree. If my husband, William, shall predecease me, my personal representative shall sell any property as to which there is no agreement within sixty days after the date of issuance of Letters of Administration concerning my estate and shall distribute the proceeds equally to my three children."

There are numerous variations of the general statement. This version limits the beneficiaries who will inherit the property—if William dies before his wife Beth—to their children who are living when Beth dies.

The children of a child who has died will inherit nothing under this provision. The purpose of limiting beneficiaries to living children is to avoid the possibility of a deceased child's share passing to a grandchild who is not yet eighteen years old (a "minor"). Having a minor inherit a fractional share of the furniture is an undesirable result. Having a minor inherit property valued in excess of $5,000 may necessitate a guardianship for the property, an even less desirable result. If Beth wants some items to go to the children of a deceased child, she can provide for such gifts in other ways. It is better not to do it in the general statement disposing of tangible personal property.

Consider including a "tie-breaker," a method of dividing the property if the beneficiaries can't agree. Common solutions are for the children to choose in order and then in reverse order or to authorize the personal representative to make the division in the event of a deadlock or to sell the disputed property and distribute the proceeds.

The Family Letter

Frequently the testator (the person making the will) wants to leave all or most of his or her tangible personal property to one beneficiary for distribution to others in accordance with instructions written as a letter from the testator to the beneficiary. In his will, William gives all his tangible personal property to Beth; however, he has also written her a letter which he has put in their safe deposit box with his will. This letter says that even though he made her the legal owner of all items of tangible personal property in his estate, he wants her to give certain items to particular people and to select at least one special memento to give to each grandchild. There is no special language or legal requirements for the letter because *it has no legal effect*. William can include any instructions he wishes. The risk is that Beth may not comply with William's instructions, possibly for reasons beyond her control. She may be in poor health and not competent to make gifts. There is *no legal obligation* on the person who inherited these assets to share them with the intended beneficiaries. If you choose this method, you are relying solely on the good faith and good intentions of the beneficiary and on the beneficiary's ability to carry out your instructions, so choose wisely and be clear in your instructions.

Two Additional Warnings

If any of the gifts to be made by the beneficiary have a value in excess of the annual exclusion from gift tax, there will be undesirable tax consequences unless the transfer can be made over several years or otherwise be made to fit within the exclusion. And if the beneficiary named in your will has any outstanding debts or obligations, creditors may be able to make claims against the property regardless of the beneficiary's good intentions.

The Legal Separate Writing

Under Florida law, a person making a will can also make a signed, separate written list of specific items of tangible personal property and the intended beneficiary of each item. If that person follows a few simple rules, the list will be enforced as part of the will. A will must refer to the separate writing, so it could contain this provision:

"If there is a separate writing signed by me and in existence at the time of my death, and if such writing is delivered to my personal representative within thirty days after the issuance of the Letter of Administration, then I give the items of tangible personal property listed in the separate writing to the persons named therein. I give all my tangible personal property, other than the items contained in my separate writing, if any, equally to my children."

Three categories of tangible personal property cannot be given away in the list: property otherwise given away under the will, property used in a trade or business, and money. Upon one's death, the separate writing becomes, in effect, a part of the will. The beauty of the separate writing is that it can be changed at any time so that if items are acquired or given away, or if a person changes his or her mind, he or she only needs to change the list. The person doesn't need to see an attorney, doesn't need to revise his or her will, and doesn't even need witnesses or a notary, though the writing must be signed and dated. However, the simplicity of this method is also its peril. Too frequently the separate writing is treated casually and, if so, it eventually causes trouble. There are three common pitfalls.

Your separate writing must be signed by you to be valid. While the law does not require it to be dated, it is a very good idea and sometimes essential. If you are completely revising a former list, destroy the former list. Catherine had a will which referred to a separate writing. During her life she prepared two different lists. When she died several years ago, both separate writings were found, both signed by Catherine, neither dated. Both documents listed almost identical assets but different beneficiaries. Needless to say, both sets of beneficiaries thought the separate writing that named them was the true, last separate writing. Only after a great deal of time and effort was it determined that one list included a few assets which were acquired later than most of the other assets and, therefore, was probably the latest list. It seemed most likely that a new list was prepared to include recently acquired items.

When preparing a separate writing, always describe both the items and the beneficiaries very specifically. It is a poor idea to say Grandmother Murphy's wedding present is to go to Bob. Not everyone will necessarily know or agree on what Grandmother gave you on your wedding day some fifty years ago. Describe each item so that even a stranger could identify it. Assume that, given half a chance, someone will misinterpret what the writing says. On the other hand, a description can be too precise. "I give my Cadillac to my son, Michael" is clear, if you still own the Cadillac at your death. What if you traded it in for a Jaguar? Who gets the Jaguar? Does Michael get anything?

The remaining concern is to ensure that your separate writing is available to be probated with your will. It should be kept with your will or with your important papers or in some other safe location so that it is not lost or destroyed without your knowledge. Additionally, your personal representative must be able to locate this precisely written, signed, and dated list. Tell your attorney, your personal representative, or a responsible family member that you have made a separate writing and where you keep it, or leave a note in your safe deposit box with your will (Don't write on your will!) disclosing the location of the separate writing. The will may say to ignore any separate writing that is not delivered to your personal representative within a specified period following your death. This provision is intended to avoid the problems that would otherwise result when your list is discovered in the bottom drawer of your desk after the desk and all your other property has been distributed to beneficiaries under your will, beneficiaries who are perhaps not the same ones set out in your separate writing.

If you want the option of making a separate writing, talk with your attorney at some length. Be sure that you understand exactly what you are supposed to do concerning the tangible personal property list, and be sure to do it.

Enumeration of Items in the Will

This is the most formal, most rigid, and most certain way of disposing of tangible personal property. If you have special items of great intrinsic value or of great personal value to you or to family members, it may be wise to list them in your will. You do not need to worry about the gifts being invalidated as a result of the technicalities and potential problems of the separate writing. Your attorney will incorporate your instructions as specific gifts in your will. These items will be inventoried and the court will see that each item goes to the beneficiary to whom it is bequeathed.

The enumeration of tangible personal property is really a form of specific gift and is often included in that section of the will, if there is one. The distinction is that a "specific gifts" provision is used to give real property and intangible personal property as well as tangible personal property.

Specific Gifts

Wills routinely contain gifts of specific property or cash amounts to an individual or organization. Frequently, real estate is specifically willed. As with tangible personal property, each item must be accurately and clearly described, taking into consideration whether the property may change during the years after the execution of your will.

Intangible Personal Property

Occasionally, an attorney is asked to include a specific gift of a stated number of shares of stock, such as "I give my 100 shares of IBM to my granddaughter, Martha." This bequest may cause problems. IBM has split and split and split and can be expected to split again. If there is a two-for-one split after you execute your will and your estate owns 200 shares, who gets the extra 100 shares? Or, what happens if you sell the stock? Does Martha get nothing or the equivalent value? If equivalent value, is it value at the time you signed the will or at the time of your death? Generally, omit the specific number of shares in gifts of stock. Your attorney can help you avoid this and other pitfalls commonly occurring with property descriptions.

Real Estate

If you want to make a specific gift of real estate, find the deed. Your attorney will need a correct legal description of the property, and the deed is the best source. Legal descriptions on a tax bill tend to be casual and sometimes inaccurate. Use your deed or perhaps your title insurance policy. Your attorney will want to review the deed to confirm how title is held whether or not the property will be a specific gift.

Consider who should receive the tangible personal property, if any, located on the property. Beth may leave the vacation home she received from her parents to her daughter, intending that the furnishings remain with the home; but Beth gave all her tangible personal property to her husband, William. William owns the furniture, the pots and pans, and the yard and pool maintenance equipment. Additionally, a gift of property should ordinarily include "all policies and proceeds of insurance covering such property."

Accurate Descriptions

Several years ago, two attorneys called me. They were stuck. Before her death, Lindsay had made a separate writing listing various items and the friends who were to receive them. Her china was given to Joan. Mary was given the balance of the tangible personal property. Joan and Mary, good friends, went to the house of their deceased friend, in the presence of the personal representative, and began to gather up the items left to each of them. Joan went into the kitchen and began to carefully pack the bowls, plates, cups, saucers, and other items of china. When she finished, she went into the living room with empty boxes, talked briefly with Mary, and began to wrap the Hummel figurines. Mary stopped her packing and said, "What are you doing, Joan?" Joan said, "These are made of china, so I am taking them." Joan and Mary probably have not spoken a civil word to each other since that hour.

Mary felt clearly that Lindsay had always wanted her to have the Hummel figurines because she herself had a collection and Lindsay knew how much she loved them. Joan thought Lindsay was being a little too emotional. Besides, the law was on her side, wasn't it? After all, they were made out of china. It was determined that, yes, the Hummel figurines were made out of china, but no, they were not "china" under the separate writing. "China" is generally thought of as a generic term for dinnerware, not as a reference to the chemical content of a particular object. In a document such as the separate writing, the usual and customary meaning was probably intended. The Hummel figurines belonged to Mary. Joan put up quite a fight before the resolution was reached, and to this day thinks the lawyers and judge unjustly deprived her of part of her rightful inheritance of "china."

Rest, Residue, and Remainder

Now that you have made specific gifts of certain property and distributed all tangible personal property, what's left is the residue. The residue may comprise the bulk of your estate or it may hold nothing. Even if you think you have given away all your property, your will should always include a provision giving away the residue, to catch any property that otherwise would not be covered and would fall into intestacy (be treated as if you did not have a will). You may have forgotten something, you may acquire additional property which does not fit into any other category in your will, a beneficiary may turn down your bequest (disclaim it), or you may fail to make sufficient alternate bequests if a beneficiary dies before you. In these cases and others, that property will pass under the intestacy (no valid will) laws unless you include a residuary gift. The residuary clause is a broad general statement: "I give and devise the rest, residue and remainder of my estate to my spouse." No items of property are named, only the beneficiary or beneficiaries to whom the broad category of property will be given.

If you didn't consider it before, think now about who should get various items in your estate if the named beneficiary is dead. Should the item go to the beneficiary's spouse or children? Should it go to another beneficiary? Should it be included in the residue? Your attorney can draft your will following your specific wishes.

Per Stirpes

Somewhere in a will you may see the words "per stirpes." Per stirpes means that the property that would have gone to a beneficiary who is dead passes down that beneficiary's family tree, generation by generation. Let's think about William and his three children: Elizabeth, with two children, Brad and Bonnie; Robert, with one child, Robert Jr.; and Blake, with two children, William II and Liz. William, a widower, leaves his estate to his children, per stirpes. Blake dies in a car accident before his father. At William's death, his estate will go one-third to Elizabeth, one-third to Robert, and Blake's one-third will be divided equally between his children, William II and Liz. If Robert had died also, Robert Jr. would get his dad's entire one-third interest, even though his cousins William II and Liz would receive only one-sixth each.

Selecting Your Personal Representative

Your attorney will ask you whom you want to name as personal representative. That is the Florida term for executor, executrix, administrator de bonis non, and the whole Latin panoply for the person (or persons) responsible for administering your estate. Administration includes locating and managing your assets, determining which claims against your estate are valid debts, paying those claims, and distributing the remainder of your estate to the proper beneficiaries.

You should give serious thought to choosing your personal representative. Most of the time, it is a spouse or a responsible family member. Like most states, Florida does have some restrictions on who can serve as personal representative: In general, the person must be a blood relative, a spouse of a blood relative, a resident of Florida, or a trust company having trust powers in Florida. Additionally, the person must be mentally and physically able to act as personal representative, must be at least eighteen years old, and must not be a felon.

If you have an existing out-of-state will which names an out-of-state bank or business associate as personal representative, it is unlikely either will be qualified to act in Florida. A few out-of-state banks have qualified in Florida and could be named personal representatives through their Florida offices. However, for the most part, your former bank and non-family members outside Florida will not be qualified. Even if your nonresident personal representative is a family member and is qualified to serve in Florida, consider your choice. All other things being equal, it is preferable to name a responsible Floridian because it is easier to administer a Florida estate from Florida. Often, in a simple estate, it is good to select a personal representative from the group of beneficiaries. These are presumably the people closest to you, and since at least part of your assets belong to them, they are more likely to be attentive to the management of the estate. However, if you think that naming one beneficiary as personal representative may create friction among any of the beneficiaries, don't do it. Go to a neutral party in whom you have trust and confidence.

Powers of a Personal Representative

The law imposes certain obligations on your personal representative (in general, to settle your estate and distribute your assets in accordance with your will and applicable law) and grants certain powers to enable him, her, or it to accomplish these tasks. Typically, a will provides additional powers so that your personal representative will have considerable authority over your estate. After all, you have carefully selected your personal representative for this position of trust. Give this person the power needed to fully manage your estate. Even in a simple will, it is advisable to give your personal representative powers in addition to those granted under the law.

The personal representative should be able to make decisions regarding tax matters, sell or otherwise deal with the real estate, and generally manage the property with broad authority to get the job done with the least amount of delay and expense. If the personal representative is not empowered to do something which needs to be done, then he or she will have to ask the probate judge for authority and explain why the particular action is necessary. It is better to provide in the will a general, broad authority, supplemented by any specific powers you anticipate may be needed, so that this additional step can be avoided, unless you believe close judicial supervision is desirable.

Real Estate Outside Florida

Special clauses are needed in the will of Floridians who own real estate outside Florida. In such cases, it is necessary to have an *ancillary administration*, which is a probate proceeding in the state where the real estate is located. Laws vary among the states, but an ancillary administration may also be required if you own personal property in another state. This probate proceeding is in addition to and subordinate to the probate proceeding in Florida. It is an abbreviated proceeding which is limited to the specific property subject to the jurisdiction of the other state. Despite this limitation, some states generate a lot of red tape if the matter of ancillary administration is not sufficiently covered in the will. The best way to handle the situation is to name a person to serve as your personal representative for the ancillary administration. Select a person who is qualified to act as personal representative under the laws of the other state and give that person the same powers and authority as your personal representative in Florida. Your ancillary personal representative and your Florida personal representative may be the same person as long as that person is qualified to act in both states.

Meeting with Your Attorney

Having given careful thought to the basic contents and requirements of a will, you are now ready to see your attorney. The attorney may have other questions, suggestions, or comments. Listen to the professional and carefully weigh any suggestions. Particularly if your attorney has considerable experience, take advantage of that experience: You are paying for it. Books and television shows may address particular matters of concern to you, but have no way of addressing, or even knowing, the factors that make your estate unique. An experienced professional who has talked with you is your best source of advice. Just as it is important for you to listen to your attorney, your attorney needs to listen to you. Tell your attorney what you want and ask questions when you don't understand. Remember, your attorney wants your estate plan to go as smoothly and simply as possibly. If your estate has problems, your attorney will have problems.

Self-Proving Wills

After your will is written and you are reading it, you may notice that there are two places for you to sign. This means your attorney is trying to make things as easy as possible for you and your personal representative. The first time you sign, you are signing as the person making the will, and your signature is evidence that this will expresses your wishes. If for any reason any part of your will is not clear to you, ask your attorney to explain.

The second time you sign, you are signing a provision that makes the will self-proving. A self-proving will can be admitted to probate without further evidence that it is eligible to be probated. No witness need appear to offer testimony. This is a considerable improvement over the way wills have been handled for the last several centuries.

How does a will become self-proving? A special affidavit is added after the end of a will. The affidavit is a notarized, sworn statement by you and the persons signing as witnesses that you, the testator, signed the document as your will, that the witnesses signed your will as witnesses, and that each of you signed the will in the presence of all of you. At the time of your death it is not necessary that the witnesses actually appear in person before the probate court. Their testimony is already incorporated in the self-proving affidavit. This allows the will to speak for itself. The process of opening administration of your estate (filing your will and certain other documents with the appropriate court) is quicker and greatly simplified. This is especially true if one or more witnesses are out of town or dead or otherwise unavailable at the time of your death.

Where Should I Keep My Will?

Now that you have made your will, what do you do with it? You might leave it with your attorney, but you probably will feel more comfortable keeping it yourself. Many people prefer to be responsible for their own papers. If you choose to keep your will, it is best to keep it in a safe deposit box. Your will can be kept with other important documents at home, in a lock-box, file cabinet, or special drawer, but it could be inadvertently thrown out or misplaced if mixed with a number of other easily accessible papers. There is also the possibility of fire or water damage.

Safe Deposit Boxes

You may have read or heard that putting your will in a safe deposit box is a bad idea because the box will be sealed by the state upon your death. Fortunately, Florida does not do this. A safe deposit box is inexpensive and is a good place to keep your important papers. Even if there is no one else's name on the box, after your death your spouse, parents, adult children, or your personal representative can open the box in the presence of a bank officer. The bank officer and the personal representative will remove the will and see that it is sent to the court.

Extra Copies

You should sign only one copy of your will. This signed document is your original will. Your attorney will make a copy of your will for you to keep at your home. The attorney will also have a copy at his or her office in your personal file. These copies are convenient since you can review the contents of your will without having to remove the original from its safe location. If you have questions or want to make a change, your attorney will have a copy readily available and can prepare any necessary revisions without the original. However, don't sign any copies.

Reviewing Your Will

I am frequently asked, "How often should I review my will?" It depends. Has there been a significant change in your life or your finances? Has the life of any beneficiary or family member changed? Have you simply had second thoughts about a prior decision? If the answer to any of these question is yes, your will may need to be revised. If your estate plan includes a more complex will, trusts, or other documents which contain specialized tax provisions, your will and these related documents should be reviewed every several years. Tax laws change constantly, and a document with significant tax language can easily go out of date. Simple wills, by virtue of their nature, are less easily outdated by changes in the law, but are just as subject to changes in personal circumstances. If children die, marry, divorce, have grandchildren, or head in the wrong direction, or if you marry or your spouse dies, it is time to look at your will and see what changes are needed.

Additionally, you need to keep in mind the initial premise under which the will was written. A 30-year-old man with a wife and two young children cannot possibly foresee how he would want his property distributed fifty years from now. He should consider and plan for his death to happen within the next five years. Then, at age 35, he should review his will and consider the next five years. A 57-year-old married woman with independent adult children may know how she wants to leave her property even if she lives to be 100. The need for regular revisions is less likely, but this doesn't mean she can put her will away and forget about it.

In this chapter, you will learn:

- what a durable power of attorney is
- who should be given your durable power of attorney
- what powers should be given
- how and why the durable power of attorney should be delivered
- who should give a durable power of attorney
- how to revoke a durable power of attorney
- when not to give a durable power of attorney
- whether to give more than one durable power of attorney

3

THE DURABLE POWER OF ATTORNEY

Many people worry that age or infirmity may cause them to become unable to manage their assets. The durable power of attorney—simple, inexpensive, and effective in a wide range of circumstances—is typically the solution, or part of the solution, for this special need. General and special powers of attorney have been in existence for a long time. A general power of attorney is a written document giving another person (referred to as your attorney-in-fact) broad authority to act for you with respect to your property. A special power of attorney gives another person (your attorney-in-fact) limited authority to perform a specific task for you. You may be familiar with these documents empowering someone to act on your behalf, but let's review how these work.

A durable power of attorney is a general power of attorney that endures the infirmity of the principal. To quote from the Florida Statutes, "This durable power of attorney shall not be affected by disability of the principal except as provided by statute." What this means, in plain English, is that if the person who signs the durable power of attorney later becomes ill, incompetent, or otherwise unable to act, the power of attorney continues to work. The person to whom the power is given (the attorney-in-fact) can assume control of the assets for the incapacitated owner.

Ordinarily, if a person is unable to manage his or her own financial resources and no one else has the necessary authority, the only solution is a guardianship. Guardianship involves a court hearing to allow a judge to decide whether the person is really unable to manage without help and, if so, to appoint a guardian. In the past, guardianships have been awkward, burdensome, expensive, and slow. Today, guardianships are more complex, more expensive, and less responsive to many of our needs. As guardianships become increasingly less desirable, the durable power of attorney becomes increasingly more significant.

You may have noticed the phrase "except as provided by statute" in the quotation above. The statute provides that a durable power of attorney remains effective until the person giving the power revokes it, dies, or is determined to be incompetent by a judge. (The durable power is suspended during the time the case is before the court. "Incompetency" is the old term which is still used in the durable power of attorney law. "Incapacity" was substituted in the guardianship laws when they were recently amended. Both terms have the same meaning.) Even if a person is clearly incompetent, the durable power continues to work until someone files a petition asking the court to determine competency. If the arrangements a person has made for the management of his or her assets prove adequate, there should be no need to have the court intervene and impose a guardianship. However, a durable power of attorney cannot guarantee against guardianship. The document may not provide sufficient authority to permit the attorney-in-fact to fully manage the incompetent person's property, the person named as attorney-in-fact may be unable or unwilling to continue to serve, or some family member may be dissatisfied with the attorney-in-fact and want to have a guardian appointed. These situations, among others, may lead to a competency hearing.

In the past, the durable power of attorney was known as a durable family power of attorney and could be given only to certain family members. The legislature believed that because the durable power grants such broad authority to the named individual, this restriction was appropriate. However, the document was so popular and worked so well to handle many matters, that the Florida legislature was persuaded to delete the family members limitation to make the document more widely available. Now Florida law permits the durable power of attorney to be given to any person, whether or not he or she is related to the giver or is a Florida resident.

More recently, the Florida legislation has increased the authority of powers of attorney. Now powers of attorney generally may not be declined to be recognized by banks, brokerage houses, or other financial institutions when the power of attorney is presented. In the past, there was sometimes a question. However, with the new Florida Statutes in place, the power of attorney is even stronger and better.

Who Should Be Named as Your Attorney-in-Fact?

The authority granted in the durable power of attorney typically is broad in scope because it is intended to provide a stand-in, another individual to act in your place with regard to your property when you are unable to do so. It should be given to a person who has exhibited maturity of judgment and wisdom in handling financial affairs and who has earned your unreserved trust and confidence. Remember, your attorney-in-fact can exercise all the broad rights and powers set forth in the durable power of attorney. You give that person the right to sign your name to legal documents relating to your property. (If you haven't already done so, turn to the durable power of attorney form in Appendix D to see what powers are typically included.) Of course, your attorney-in-fact has a legal obligation to use the durable power of attorney in good faith and only to serve your best interests. (This is known as a fiduciary obligation.) He or she is not authorized to use the powers for personal gain or contrary to your intent or your best interests.

What Should the Durable Power of Attorney Say?

Under the law, the property subject to a durable power of attorney includes all property that you own, whether real estate, stocks and bonds, bank accounts, or any other kind of real and personal property. Even your interest in any jointly held property is subject to the durable power. The specific language of your durable power of attorney determines what authority your attorney-in-fact may exercise over this property. You are trying to cover all major bases here. Many unforeseen factors can arise in your financial life and, ordinarily, you want your attorney-in-fact to be able to address these matters if you cannot.

One power which you want to consider and which is not included in the form in Appendix D is the power to make gifts. Gift making by an attorney-in-fact is a very difficult subject. When should the holder of the power of attorney make a gift of your assets if you are incapacitated and unable to express your own wishes? How much should be given away? To whom should gifts be made? What assets should be given? Clearly this can be a fertile area of controversy. The person who holds the power to make gifts may make gifts to himself or herself. Other interested persons can challenge such gifts on the grounds that the gifts were not part of the overall estate plan but were made simply to benefit the recipient. The court may void the challenged gifts if it determines that the holder of the power of attorney abused his or her power or if it finds that the holder cannot show that his or her acts benefited the person who gave the power of attorney.

The power to make gifts should be included in a durable power of attorney only when it is clear that the gifts will be advantageous to the donor and the donor's estate plan and that they are unlikely to cause major controversy within the family or with other beneficiaries. If it is desirable to permit the holder of the durable power to make gifts, then the document must include language specifically granting that right.

Conditions of Delivery

Your durable power of attorney is not effective unless it is "delivered" while you are competent. Signing the durable power of attorney document does not make the person you named in that document your attorney-in-fact. "Delivery" requires that you give both the document and all the authority which goes with the document to your attorney-in-fact.

If Scott gives Carol a durable power of attorney but tells her she could not use it unless he called her, he would have made a conditional delivery. If Scott had left the document in his office desk and never gave it to Carol, the durable power would not have been delivered. If Scott became incapacitated before he gave the document to Carol, the durable power would remain undelivered and would be ineffective.

Postponing delivery, either by making a conditional delivery or by keeping control of the document, is possible but not recommended. It is especially unwise if anyone is likely to challenge the durable power of attorney. Your attorney-in-fact will need to prove not only that you delivered the durable power but also that you were competent at the time of the delivery. It is best to give the document to your attorney-in-fact shortly after you have signed it, rather than to keep it and expect that he or she will able to find it and use it later. Just as you must trust your attorney-in-fact to use the durable power only for your benefit, you must trust him or her to use it only when it is necessary. It is very important to select a person you can expect not to abuse your trust.

Revocation

The person who gives the durable power of attorney can revoke it at any time. It also can be revoked by court order. It is always revoked by death. Upon death, the will, a trust, or whatever documents provide for the disposition of assets come into effect.

You may revoke the durable power of attorney either by having the durable power of attorney document returned to you and destroying it or by giving your attorney-in-fact a written statement that you are revoking it. As a practical matter you may wish to do more. You may even send a copy of the notice of revocation to everyone who knew about the durable power and might otherwise assume your former attorney-in-fact still has authority to act for you. If the durable power may be used in any manner affecting real property, or if it was recorded for any reason, and if you are concerned it still might be used, record a copy of the revocation in the county in which you own real estate or where any prior power of attorney was recorded.

Who Should Give a Durable Power of Attorney?

While the durable power of attorney can be a valuable estate-planning tool, it is not necessary in all situations. It grants broad powers and should not be used indiscriminately. For a young couple with little likelihood of incapacity, the durable power of attorney may not appear to be particularly useful. However, even young couples may need a durable power of attorney for special circumstances, as when one spouse is going to be out of the country for an extended period of time, perhaps serving in the military or working for a multinational corporation. Here, the durable power of attorney can be extremely helpful in letting the spouse who remains at home transact the financial affairs of the couple without relying on the slow, overseas mail. In today's world, even with our modern communications, it can take an extended period of time for written documents to go to some countries and to be returned. The financial world moves much faster than overseas mail. Facsimile machines quickly transmit pages of information over long distances, but you can't get an original executed document over the fax line. Many transactions require the real thing, not a copy. Without a power of attorney, any check that requires both spouses' signatures has to travel between spouses. Faxing a check for the absent spouse to sign and deposit (or sign and fax back) won't work.

For the older couple, the durable power of attorney is almost essential. Faced with the increasing likelihood of incapacitating illness and the delay and expense involved in guardianships, the durable power of attorney should always be considered. This document is not always the right choice, however.

When Not to Give a Durable Power of Attorney

A durable power of attorney may not work well in certain situations. Trying to operate an active business for a long period of time under a durable power of attorney is not ideal, nor is managing properties located in several states. A more common example occurs in many second marriages made late in life. Either or both spouses may have adult children from a prior marriage. They may have signed a nuptial agreement in which both spouses limit or waive their respective marital rights in the other's assets. Giving each other a durable power of attorney in this situation is usually not wise. If one spouse (Kristy) becomes incapacitated, the other spouse (Bob) is in a difficult position. Even if Bob is a capable, fair individual who previously got along well with Kristy's children, exercising his authority as attorney-in-fact can be a burden on him and a source of conflict. The children feel protective toward their mother. They may be suspicious of Bob's motives, and, not infrequently, they may disagree with his decisions. These conflicting opinions can lead to misunderstanding, family friction, and in some instances, outright rifts. For these reasons, it is frequently better to give the durable power of attorney to an older son or daughter rather than a new spouse.

Should You Give More Than One Durable Power of Attorney?

The durable power of attorney is nondelegable. This means that if you give the power of attorney to someone, that person may not in turn pass that power of attorney on to someone else of his or her choice, even if he or she becomes unable or unwilling to act for you. Only the person who receives the power of attorney from you can exercise it. You can, however, provide in the power of attorney an alternate or backup person to exercise the power of attorney if your first choice is unable or unwilling to serve any longer.

Nondelegability is one reason it may be desirable to give more than one person your durable power of attorney. No restriction in the law prohibits this. It is possible to give the durable power of attorney to both a spouse and a child or to two children, for example. Dividing responsibility, pooling business judgment, instituting a system of checks and balances, and simply avoiding a choice among qualified close family members are additional reasons for not limiting your choice to a single individual.

For example, Bill and Marge are getting on in years. They have two sons, Bob and Charles, and a modest estate. Bill is concerned about what will happen if he is no longer able to manage the family assets. Marge has never wanted to deal with any of the financial aspects of their life. She doesn't even like to write checks. Bill and Marge have a great deal of confidence in their sons and know that Bob and Charles will want to help if something should happen to either of them. Bill and Marge decided that each of them should sign a durable power of attorney appointing the other as attorney-in-fact. Each of them is now able to act for both of them in any transaction concerning their property. If Marge's signature is needed, Bill can use the durable power of attorney to sign her name as her attorney-in-fact. Perhaps Marge is concerned about assuming responsibility if Bill becomes unable to manage the family finances. She is pleased that the durable power of attorney will make the transition easier. Additionally, Bill and Marge thought it was a good idea to give durable powers of attorney to their sons. If Bill becomes seriously ill, Marge will want to spend her time with him, not coping with their financial affairs. Bob and Charles could use the durable powers of attorney to help their parents during this period. Either of them could raise money for their father's medical expenses or change the investments to produce a higher income stream or just attend to routine financial matters.

A durable power of attorney can be structured to require both Bob and Charles to act together to exercise its authority. This serves as a check in that each one must get the consent of the other before the durable power of attorney can be used. If one person exercises bad judgment, the other can refuse to go along. However, there is a negative side. A recalcitrant coholder of the durable power of attorney can block good decisions. From a practical standpoint, it may be inconvenient to require the holders to act together, since both must then sign every document. You can best decide whether the holders of your durable power of attorney should be required to act together, or whether you want each to have the power to act individually.

There is another side of this question of multiple powers to be considered. Many banks, stock brokerage firms, and other institutions have their own durable power of attorney forms they prefer to be used. Even if you only want to name one individual as your attorney-in-fact, it may be more effective to sign several different bank or brokerage house forms to ensure that the individual can completely manage all your property without unnecessary complications.

Typically, powers of attorney deal with financial matters—handling assets, signing legal documents, managing property, and so forth. Now, under Florida law, the holder of a durable power of attorney may be given authority "to arrange for and consent to medical, therapeutic, and surgical procedures for the principal, including the administration of drugs." (The "principal" is the person who gave the durable power.) This provision is a significant shift into an area previously closed to power holders. The new durable power of attorney may be given to a person you authorize to make important health care decisions for you, as well as to manage your property. Typically, however, a durable power of attorney for health decisions will be a separate document from the durable power of attorney for financial matters.

The durable power of attorney for medical matters—along with the living will and the designation of health care surrogate—will be discussed further in Chapter 4. It seems wisest to address medical decisions separately from financial decisions. For this reason, the form of a durable power of attorney appearing in Appendix D does not contain language specifically relating to medical, therapeutic, or surgical procedures. The grant of authority for medical powers is contained in the health care advance directive form found in Appendix E.

Summary

The durable power of attorney, combining simplicity and broad authority, is one of the most frequently used estate planning tools. It is also one of the least expensive. Florida attorneys who handle estate planning have a standard form for a durable power of attorney. They also keep a file of optional provisions which are commonly used. Even custom-tailoring a durable power of attorney to address a special concern or asset that you own is rarely time consuming. The document is created by selecting appropriate provisions from the existing collection of alternate provisions and adding or substituting them into a standard form. The power to make gifts is one example of an optional provision. The power to consent to medical, therapeutic, and surgical procedures is another.

Whether the attorney uses a preprinted form or a tailor-made power of attorney, the power of attorney is very inexpensive for what it does. It is easy to understand and implement. When you start your estate planning, you should consider the durable power of attorney.

In this chapter, you will learn:

- what is included in a written or oral living will
- how to give instructions about feeding tubes
- how a living will works
- if a living will covers you outside of Florida
- how a living will is signed
- how to revoke a living will
- the medical power of attorney and health care surrogate
- who should and should not be named as your surrogate

4

LIVING WILLS

Few decisions are more difficult, more traumatic, and more painful than the decision a family must make for the medical care of a loved one who can be kept alive only by artificial means. In one of the most well-known cases in American law, the New Jersey Supreme Court wrote:

"Medicine, with its combination of advanced technology and professional ethics, is both able and inclined to prolong biological life. Law, with its felt obligation to protect the life and freedom of the individual, seeks to assure each person's right to live out his human life until its natural and inevitable conclusion. Theology, with its acknowledgment of man's dissatisfaction with biological life as the ultimate source of joy . . . defends the sacredness of human life and defends it from all attack."

In re Quinlan

The dramatic dilemma faced by law, medicine, and the family of Karen Ann Quinlan was played out as our society and that family sought to find their way through what is now known as the "right to die."

43

Responding to this case and cases within its borders, Florida adopted the "Life Prolonging Procedure Act," a policy statement on an adult's right to die. The law permits an adult to make the written declaration commonly known as a living will.

Florida believes that every competent adult has the fundamental right to control the decisions relating to his or her own medical care. This right includes the decision to have provided, withheld, or withdrawn medical procedures that could prolong life. Each individual's right is subject to society's interest in protecting human life. However, while recognizing the sanctity of life, Florida also recognizes that artificially prolonging the life of a person with a terminal condition may provide only a precarious and burdensome existence and may not provide what is medically necessary or beneficial for the patient.

The Written and the Oral Living Will

The Florida statutes provide for both oral and written declarations. The oral declaration may be made only if the patient is physically unable to sign a written declaration. If so, the patient's statement is put into writing and one of the witnesses who heard it signs the patient's signature in the patient's presence and at the patient's direction. Additionally, the oral statement may be made only *after* the diagnosis of a terminal condition. This imposes some severe restraints on the use of oral declarations. People who feel strongly about terminating medical care should prepare a written declaration before the need arises. The law offers a suggested form for the written declaration which is shown in Appendix F.

How a Living Will Works

You may wonder if the hospitals and doctors in Florida really recognize the living will. The answer is yes. The medical care providers must determine that the person is terminal and that death is imminent. Once the determination is made that a person is terminal and death is imminent, the living will becomes part of the medical record. The response in almost every case is to follow the law which provides for withdrawal of medical procedures to prolong life. In fact, if a physician chooses not to comply with the living will, then the physician is required to make a reasonable effort to transfer the patient to another physician. In practice, a transfer is not needed very often. A physician usually accepts the living will unless there are circumstances which cause him or her to feel that it is not a valid document, that the person is not terminal, or that death is not imminent. "Terminal" as defined in the statute means: (a) a condition caused by injury, disease, or illness from which there is no reasonable probability of recovery and which, without treatment, can be expected to cause death; or (b) a persistent vegetative state characterized by a permanent and irreversible condition of unconsciousness in which there is: (1) the absence of voluntary action or cognitive behavior of any kind; and (2) an inability to communicate or interact purposefully with the environment.

What If I Become Ill Outside of Florida?

While the Florida living will is valid here, not all states may recognize Florida living wills. While most states have some form of law providing for living wills, the language and requirements vary from state to state. Nevertheless, the Florida living will should provide guidance as to the wishes of the terminally ill person. Most health care providers, even outside of Florida, will consider such wishes.

Feeding Tubes

One of the most troubling questions has been whether to withdraw water and food. The Florida law speaks of withdrawing life-prolonging procedures, which are currently defined as mechanical or other artificial means—such as a respirator and feeding tubes—that are used to sustain or restore vital function. Feeding tubes were added to the living will law when the Florida Supreme Court ruled in the dramatic and touching case of *Estelle Browning*. Estelle had seen a friend placed on feeding tubes. Afterwards, Estelle specifically provided in her living will that she was not to have feeding tubes. Tragically, Estelle suffered a stroke and was placed on feeding tubes—the very thing she feared most. Florida statutes at that time did not provide for feeding tubes to be withdrawn pursuant to a living will. Estelle's case found its way to the Florida Supreme Court. The court ruled that she had a fundamental right of privacy and, based on that right, she could direct that feeding tubes be withdrawn.

The Florida constitutional right of privacy as interpreted here means more than privacy in general terms. In this context, it means liberty or freedom from state interference. It implies a fundamental right of self-determination. The Florida Supreme Court stated:

"Today we hold that, without prior judicial approval, a surrogate or proxy, as provided here, may exercise the constitutional right of privacy for one who has become incompetent and who, while competent, expressed his or her wishes orally or in writing. We also determine that there is no legal distinction between gastrostomy or nasogastric feeding and any other means of life support. This case resolves a question of an individual's constitutional right of self-determination. We are hopeful that this decision will encourage those who want their wishes to be followed to express their wishes clearly and completely."

When the Supreme Court of Florida announced its decision in the *Browning* case, the Florida legislature rapidly wrote new laws concerning health care for people who are incapacitated and unable to express their wishes. The result was three legal documents in the statutes that govern when a person is unable to express his or her own wishes. They are the living will, designation of medical surrogate, and durable power of attorney for medical care.

The law was amended in 1990 to cover those who wished a nasal/gastric tube not be used or, if used, withdrawn. Florida law in regard to living wills is still evolving. It is not fixed in place but is a living, growing response to society and its perception of what is proper and ethical. Florida is recognizing that people have a valid constitutional right to express their wishes concerning their health care if they are terminal and to reasonably expect that those wishes will be honored when the time comes.

Formality of Signing

The living will does not need to be notarized. It does require two witnesses who are not related to or married to the person signing the living will. You should sign several copies of your living will. (This is referred to as "making multiple originals.") Keep one signed copy at home and give one to your physician. A signed copy should be given to a sibling or an adult child, and an additional signed copy may be kept in an easily located place.

Revocation

You may revoke your living will declaration. This is done by a signed and dated revocation, by physical cancellation, by destruction of the written declaration, or by an oral expression of intent to revoke the declaration when communicated to the attending physician.

From a practical standpoint, if a person does not want heroic or extended life-prolonging procedures to be used, that person should execute a living will. If the statutory form expresses your wishes, then follow the form. Departure from this form might, in some instances, cause the declaration to be invalidated and, in almost all instances, will cause the care providers to proceed more slowly and more carefully than they would with the familiar statutory form.

No one should ever feel obligated to sign a living will declaration. It is a very personal, individual decision. Many people, when considering the prospect of medical care during a terminal illness, want everything to be done for as long as possible. Someone else may say, "Don't put me on those machines." Another will respond, "I have no intention of dying, and I think the whole question is irrelevant. I refuse to consider it any further." The decision can be difficult because it involves contemplating one's own mortality. As one of the sages said, "It's not so much death I fear, as the prospect of dying."

The Medical Surrogate

The Florida legislature provided a very extensive, detailed statute—similar to a power of attorney—for a person acting as an agent on another's behalf regarding the giving of medical care. The medical surrogate statute provides for the designation through a health care advance directive of an individual or individuals who are to make medical decisions for an incapacitated person. Unlike the living will, the appointment of a medical surrogate comes into effect immediately. It is not necessary that the person be determined to be terminal or that death be imminent, as in the living will. This is one of the essential differences between medical care surrogate and the living will. The medical care surrogate is authorized to make medical decisions which cover almost every conceivable question or situation that may arise. Not only can medical care surrogates make medical care decisions, but they also can consult with health care providers and provide what is known as "informed consent." They are specifically authorized to give medical consents, authorizations, or releases; to access any clinical records or other medical information; to apply for benefits such as Medicare and Medicaid; and to transfer an individual to or from a hospital, hospice, nursing home, or other care facility.

The health care surrogate has the right to receive information concerning the diagnosis, prognosis, alternative treatments, risks versus benefits of treatment, side effects of any medication, financial impact of proposed treatment, and the likely outcome if consent is not given with regard to all suggested treatments.

The person who designates a medical surrogate may revoke the designation at any time. Like the power of attorney, it can be revoked in writing or by recovering the written surrogate form.

Who Should Be Named as a Health Care Surrogate?

The person (or persons) you name as your health care surrogate should be someone you would want to make medical decisions for you, usually a spouse or a child. It is possible to name a number of people in series so that if one were unable to make medical decisions for some reason, another would be named as the alternate. It is also quite common to name two persons simultaneously. This is done to avoid hard feelings or questions as to why one person was named and not another.

Who Should Not Be Designated as a Health Care Surrogate?

A person does not have to be related to you to be a surrogate, but he or she must be at least eighteen years old. Also, the surrogate should be someone other than your doctor or other health care provider, or any employee or relative of your doctor or health care provider.

What Happens if I Don't Name a Health Care Surrogate?

.If you do not name a health care surrogate and you become incapacitated, then either your health care facility or a court will designate a person to act on your behalf. Usually, this will be a spouse, child, parent, or someone closely related to you. What if you sign a health care surrogate designating your spouse as your health care surrogate and then later you divorce? In that instance, the divorce, upon becoming final, would revoke the health care surrogate designation. You then should designate another person to serve as your health care surrogate.

The Form for Designation of Health Care Surrogate and Medical Power of Attorney

Included in Appendix E is a health care advance directive form which is used for a combined designation of health care surrogate and durable medical power of attorney. This is just one of many forms these documents might take. The two forms have been combined into one here to make them easier to use and to take advantage of the best aspects of each form. The health care advance directive form is excellent because it is detailed and specific in the medical powers given. The form in this book attempts to provide a combined designation of health care surrogate and living will. The language may be changed to reflect a person's wishes.

Summary

The difficult, confusing, and highly emotionally charged area of medical care for an incapacitated person has been the subject of considerable attention from the courts and from the legislature. Gradually, the courts and the legislature, as well as society in general, seem to be moving toward a feeling that people may clearly express how they wish medical decisions to be made for them if, at some later date, they cannot speak for themselves. Starting with the cases of *Karen Ann Quinlan*, *Nancy Cruzan*, and the more recent (1997) Supreme Court cases of *Vacco vs. Quill* and *Worthington vs. Glucksberg*, federal and state courts are setting standards regarding the "right to die" and the right to palliative or pain management care. In the Florida case of *Estelle Browning* and others, the courts have said that a person has the right to set forth how his or her medical care is to be handled and that all Floridians have a constitutional right to expect that those wishes will be carried out.

The Florida legislature has responded to these opinions by providing guidelines for how a person's statements are to be set forth and recognized. The legislature has set forth statutory provisions. The living will expresses a person's wishes if he or she is terminal and death is imminent. The designation of a health care surrogate is specific concerning medical care. Both of these documents respond to society's feelings concerning medical care, and each gives us the right to express our wishes beforehand about how we want our medical care to be handled in the event we become incapacitated.

In this chapter, you will learn:

- the pros and cons of trusts
- how incompetency is determined
- the disadvantage of guardianships
- how to avoid probate
- what fees to expect
- how to save on estate taxes
- what income taxes to expect after death
- what marital rights are
- deeding real estate into a living trust
- whether trusts are private
- what the living trust document provides
- how distributions are made
- what powers a trustee has
- what a successor trustee is
- what a corporate trustee is
- how to fund your trust
- how to decide if a living trust is right for you

5

LIVING TRUSTS

For many years, living trusts have been a cornerstone in constructing estate plans for Floridians. It has been more than 30 years since Norman Dacey came out with his now famous book entitled "How to Avoid Probate." That book, and the thoughts expressed in it, struck a responsive chord with the public. Since that time, the living trust, also known as the revocable trust, has been increasingly popular. A living trust—known also as an *inter vivos* trust or a self-declaration trust—may generally be described as a trust set up by an individual while he or she is alive. The individual frequently names himself or herself as trustee but may alternatively name a bank or another individual to serve as trustee. Under the terms of the living trust, the person who creates it receives the income and as much principal as he or she may request at any time. The trust is completely revocable and may be changed by the person who set it up. In short, the person creating the trust places most of his or her property into the trust but loses no control over his or her assets. While there are many types of trusts, this is the pattern most living trusts follow.

By the time we finish this chapter, you will have a good idea about what a living trust is and whether it's a good idea for you. Not all people—and certainly not all attorneys—will agree with everything expressed in this book. Many will disagree with the opinions in this chapter. Nevertheless, if you remember that a living trust is neither a cure-all nor a complex, expensive, frustrating fraud, you will be able to make your own decisions, and those decisions will be the right ones for you.

Unfortunately, many laypersons view the living trust as a panacea for all estate planning problems. They believe it will save estate taxes, reduce the cost of probate, and speed up administration of the estate. They believe it will keep creditors from claiming against the estate and protect the estate against will contests, greedy heirs, and overreaching attorneys. Conversely, many attorneys, even some in the estate planning field, view the living trust with suspicion. They overreact to the unwarranted expectations of the public by telling their clients that living trusts are unwise, inefficient, expensive, clumsy, difficult to deal with, full of red tape, illegal, and confusing. The living trust will not solve all ills, but it can be beneficial and even essential in many estate planning situations. For a brief summary of fact and fiction about living trusts, see page 53.

Let's look at some of the reasons for using a living trust. The living trust may provide a good vehicle for current management of assets. Many people, for various reasons, do not want to manage their own assets. They may be elderly or infirm, or their lives may be so occupied by their jobs that they do not have time to spend on managing these assets. Professionals may find themselves in this situation, as do entertainers and people who are required to be out of the country for extended periods.

COMPARISON OF WILLS AND LIVING TRUSTS

	Will	**Living Trust**
Estate tax savings	Same as a living trust	Same as a will
Income tax savings savings	No significant income tax savings	No significant income tax savings
Costs to settle the estate	Usually 1%–2% more than with a trust	Usually saves 1%–2% over a will (probate)
Distributions to beneficiary	Distributions can be made as promptly as with a living trust	Distributions can be made as promptly as with a will
Confidentiality and privacy of documents	Private before death; public after death	Semiprivate both before and after death
Confidentiality of assets	Private before and after death	Private before and after death
Incompetency	No benefit if incompetent	Considerable benefit if incompetent
Creditor protection	Protection after three months	No protection until two years
Costs to create document	Cheaper than a living trust	More expensive than a will

Many times someone will ask a trust department to manage assets in an investment program. The trust department may do this through an investment management account. The person remains his or her own trustee, or at times the corporate investment adviser may be asked to become the trustee under the terms of the trust agreement to buy, sell, and otherwise make investments.

The Living Trust

What is it? As defined earlier in this chapter, the living trust is an agreement set up while the person is alive. The trust agreement defines who the trustee is and what the trustee's obligations will be. Assets are put in the trust, and the trustee follows the instructions written in the trust agreement. The trust agreement actually is a contract between two people: One is the person who puts the assets into the trust and the other is the trustee. Some living trusts are 40 pages long. Others are 15. The length depends upon the complexity of the estate planning situation and on the participants' feelings as to what is most appropriate. This changes from one client to another and from one attorney to another.

Ingredients

Let us consider what the typical ingredients of a living trust are. First, the trust agreement will identify the person putting assets into the trust. Generally this person is known as the grantor, the settlor, and sometimes the trustor. This is the person creating the trust; typically, this would be you.

The trustee is the person who receives the assets, invests them, and distributes the income and principal according to the grantor's (your) wishes. The trust must specifically provide that it can be altered, amended, or revoked in any way that you as the grantor see fit.

Distributions

The trust normally will provide that all the trust income will be distributed to you and that you may take out as much principal as you wish on demand. The trust will provide that if you become incapacitated, the trustee has the power to distribute income and, if necessary, principal to others on your behalf. In the event you become incapacitated, the trustee can use funds to pay for nursing care, nursing homes, extended-care facilities, hospitals, and physicians, as well as day-to-day living expenses. Some trusts go further and provide that the trustee may distribute principal or income to a spouse. The thinking here is that if all the assets of the family are in the trust and all income will be held by the trustee for the benefit of the grantor, this may leave the grantor's spouse and family in a difficult situation. Fortunately, Florida law is not that harsh, but it probably is a wise idea to have a clause in the trust saying that the assets in the trust may be used for the benefit of either the grantor or the grantor's spouse.

Upon the death of the grantor, the trust typically says that the trustee is authorized to pay the debts of the deceased, pay any estate taxes, transmit funds to the personal representative for the purposes of these costs or other expenses, and hold the remaining assets in the trust according to specified terms and conditions.

Upon the death of the person creating a living trust, the terms and conditions of the trust may be as broad as human imagination can be, subject to a few limitations. These limitations are imposed chiefly as a matter of public policy. Frequently, a living trust provides that the income will go to the surviving spouse. If the spouse is dead, the trust may provide that the principal will go to the children. Sometimes, if the children are young, the trust provides that the trustee will continue to hold the income or principal in the trust and to distribute only as much income or principal as is necessary for a child's health, support, maintenance, or education, taking into consideration other assets which may be otherwise available to the child. The distribution of the principal would occur in stages specified by the grantor.

Trustee Powers

What is income? What is principal? What types of investments are permissible for the trustee to use? Giving a trustee wide latitude usually turns out to be better than setting narrow limits. When considering what trust powers the trustee should have, most people are naturally inclined to be conservative, and conservatism is generally a desirable thing in the area of estate planning. Here, however, too much conservatism can be a problem. It is impossible to look into the future and see what types of investments, opportunities, or problems will occur during the lifetime of the trust. Because of this, it is generally wiser to give much broader discretion to the trustee than might be considered appropriate initially.

There are two other reasons that it is desirable to give a trustee broad discretionary powers. First, because trustees are required by Florida law to manage trusts in a conservative fashion, they will be naturally conservative. Secondly, trustees are required to adhere to what is known as a fiduciary responsibility. A fiduciary responsibility is the highest kind of responsibility that can be imposed on an individual. Because the fiduciary responsibility is so strong and the courts are so strict regarding trustees, trustees will naturally gravitate toward safe ground. Usually, problems arising in the trustee's powers are a result of too narrow rather than too broad a grant of authority.

Successor Trustees

In the *inter vivos* area, it is common that the trustee of the living trust is the person who created the trust. Successor trustees should also be named in the trust. If the grantor becomes incapacitated through age, illness, death, or misfortune, someone else can manage the assets in accordance with the terms of the trust. Generally you, as the person creating the trust, will know who will be best able to manage your assets if you are unable to look after them yourself. Sometimes it is a spouse. Sometimes it is a trusted friend or professional adviser or a trust company. Frequently, it is a child or maybe two children. After all, there is no requirement to have only one trustee. If you have more than two trustees, however, things are going to be more complicated. It can be inefficient and clumsy if, for example, each check must be signed by all trustees.

Corporate Trustees

Corporate trustees fulfill a very necessary function in the field of estate planning. Their trust officers have special knowledge about how to administer trusts and interpret instructions given in trust agreements. However, not all corporate trustees are created equal, nor are all trust officers created equal. In fact, the corporate trustee you name today may be owned by another corporation next year.

The banking industry has changed a great deal over the past 20 years, and according to industry analysts, it is likely that change will continue over the next 20 years. These changes directly affect trust departments and the administration of trusts in terms of efficiency, responsiveness, operating procedures, and expenses. You may want an individual and a corporate trustee to serve together. Each brings special skills to the relationship: the individual brings the personal touch, and the corporate trustee, technical knowledge.

Fees for Corporate Trustees

Some trust departments quote fees based on the amount of principal plus a different percentage of income depending on the services requested. Others choose to give a more generalized rate. Still others charge for each transaction that occurs in the trust. A general rule of thumb is that it is probably going to cost about 1% of the value of the principal to have the trust run by a corporate fiduciary each year. If you calculate 1% of all the assets that might be in the trust and then consider that this figure will be taken out of the trust each year for as long the corporate trustee will serve, you will see that it can become very expensive over the long term. Yet the corporate trustee is usually a stable financial institution. Corporate trustees also argue that they have better investment results and keep better records than individuals. Many do; some do not. By and large, most corporate trustees are here to stay, meet a special need, and provide dependable service to their customers.

Funding Your Trust

Once you have set the terms of the trust and it has been prepared, reviewed, and signed, you need to place your assets into the trust. The importance of putting assets into the trust cannot be overemphasized. All too frequently, people will spend considerable sums of money to establish a trust and then fail to put assets into it. This is not unlike the person who buys a very expensive automobile and never puts gas into it. See Appendix G for instructions on funding a trust.

Incompetency

It is desirable to consider an *inter vivos* trust as an alternative to guardianship for future management of the assets if incompetency might arise. Florida law concerning guardianships has changed. Many new provisions have been added which greatly increase the cost and "red tape" of guardianships. Because of the possibility of accident, age, or illness, you may be concerned about managing your assets. You can set up a living trust which provides that you will manage assets as long as you can. If you are unable to do so, you have already named a successor trustee to take over. If a trust with a successor trustee has not been created, the court probably will appoint a guardian for the property. By having a trust that specifically names a successor trustee, you can be sure the question "Who shall manage my assets if I am incapacitated or incompetent?" is settled.

Suppose Frank is in his seventies and is wondering how he should set up his estate plan. His attorney recommends a living trust. Having considered the benefits of a living trust, Frank agrees, and the attorney prepares a trust. Under the terms of the trust, Frank is his own trustee. He can alter, amend, revoke, or change the trust in any way he wishes as long as he is alive and competent to do so. He receives all the income under the terms of the trust and receives as much of the principal as he wishes.

As trustee, he controls investment decisions completely. If he becomes incapacitated, Frank has named in the trust his son, Bill, to take over as his successor trustee. The successor trustee, of course, has the responsibility of paying the income and, if necessary, principal, for Frank's benefit. If Frank were severely incapacitated, he might be in a nursing home. Bill could pay income directly to the nursing home. If Frank had to have a significant operation, Bill could pay the doctors and hospital as well. Because Frank's assets are already in his trust, it would not be necessary to appoint a formal court-supervised guardian for Frank's assets. Bill could just take over managing these assets as Frank's successor trustee. Bill, however, would not have the power to alter, amend, or revoke the trust. That is reserved only for the creator of the trust.

On Frank's death, the assets in the trust are distributed by Bill to the beneficiaries. The assets are still subject to estate taxes; they are not increased or decreased by the trust. The settlement of Frank's estate will not be speeded up or slowed down because of the trust if the assets are over the exempt amount, because the IRS will not permit an estate to be closed until the agency has reviewed the estate tax return and issued its "closing letter."

On the other hand, if Frank's assets are under the exempt amount, then Bill may choose to distribute the assets in the trust promptly. He might decide to hold off until all the bills are in, or he might distribute part of the assets and then hold back a small reserve in case unexpected expenses arise.

If Frank did not feel that his son, Bill, was the right person to handle funds due to Bill's age or lack of experience in handling assets, Frank could designate some other person or, if there wasn't any other person Frank felt was appropriate, Frank could name a trust department. The trust department would pay Frank's bills, handle the investments, and ultimately distribute assets to the beneficiaries Frank had chosen.

All in all, this is a fairly simple process and one which is used in Florida every day.

Guardianships

There is another advantage to a living trust when it comes to the future management of property. Not only does the living trust provide *who* shall serve as the person to manage these assets, but, more specifically and more importantly, it also defines *how* these assets shall be managed. The alternative to the living trust is a guardianship. There are few attorneys today who would advocate a guardianship over a living trust. Guardianships in Florida are very expensive and time-consuming. The process involves the testimony of physicians, friends, and family, and a considerable amount of attorney time, court time, expense, and perhaps family embarrassment.

Once a judge determines that a person is unable to manage his or her affairs, the court appoints an individual or a corporation to serve as guardian. The guardian is subject to a great number of restrictions and requirements. Each one causes more expense, more delay, and more red tape. Under a living trust, on the other hand, assets are easily administered by the successor trustee. If there is a situation where there is a reasonable likelihood that a person may become incapacitated, it is wise to consider a living trust for the future management of assets.

Avoiding Probate

The most common reason for setting up a living trust is avoiding probate. Many people's perceptions concerning probate in Florida are based on what they have experienced in northern states. Florida probate is as different from the procedures in New York, Massachusetts, Michigan, and other states as our Florida winter is different from their winter. Florida probate functions relatively quickly and inexpensively compared to most northern states. An example of the differences may be seen in the fees charged by trust departments, depending upon whether the estate is administered through a trust or through a probate proceeding.

Fees

The difference between the cost of probate and that of trusts is generally far less than many people think. After estate taxes are considered, the difference may be less than 1% of the value of the estate assets. After estate taxes in the 37% to 55% range—or income taxes in the 30% range—are considered, the difference may be less than 1/2 of 1%. Not much difference. You should take the opportunity to discuss the savings with your estate-planning attorney. Frequently the savings for a trust will be far less than predicted by well-intentioned stock brokers, life insurance salesmen, or other people purporting to have some knowledge of these matters.

Avoiding the Delay of Probate

As we will see in Chapter 17, probate is a process whereby assets passing under a will through court supervision are distributed to beneficiaries.

Assets passing through probate may encounter delays due to several factors. One is the process of determining assets and beneficiaries. Occasionally, problems arise in determining what assets are in the estate and who will receive them. This kind of delay can occur in either a will or a trust. However, if the assets and beneficiaries are clearly identified, these problems can be avoided whether the assets are passing under a will or through a trust.

Another type of delay arises when the personal representative does not want to distribute assets until the creditor's claim period or the period for contesting the will has elapsed. This is usually three months after the probate process has started. Trustees frequently will want a court proceeding to eliminate possible creditor claims. Sometimes, trustees will distribute assets within this three-month period. Some problems that arise in wills are also being seen with trusts as trusts grow in popularity. For instance, people are taking exception to the disposition of assets in trusts just as they take exception to the disposition of assets in wills. As a result, trustees are becoming more cautious about distributing assets. Personal representatives frequently can be encouraged to give partial early distributions from an estate rather than wait for the full three-month period. Thus, some estate planning professionals feel that there is a gradual merging of the probate process and the trust administration process after one's death. This seems to be the clear trend.

Still another type of delay in settling estates arises because of estate taxes. Here there is no difference between the estate tax treatment of wills and of trusts. The IRS reviews all estate tax returns. The final closing of a person's estate filing an estate tax return—whether passing via a will or a trust—does not occur until the IRS issues what is known as a "closing letter." In it, the IRS says that it has examined the estate tax return, that it is satisfied with the return, and that all assets have been reported and all taxes due have been paid. This letter comes just as slowly whether the estate is passing under a will or a trust.

On balance, it seems that assets now are distributed just as promptly under a trust as under a will. Trustees, seeing litigation against other trustees, are now a bit slower to distribute assets shortly after the death of the decedent. Personal representatives acting under wills are more responsive to the wishes and needs of the beneficiaries than they have been in the past.

Saving Estate Taxes

Occasionally, people will be encouraged to enter into a living trust to save estate taxes. The claim that a living trust saves taxes over a will may be clearly and simply answered: "Horsefeathers!" Living trusts do not save estate taxes any more than a wills do. The IRS does not care whether assets are inherited via a living trust or a will.

Income Taxes after Death

When it comes to income taxes, the living trust is neutral. Occasionally, people think that living trusts will save them income taxes. Under the tax changes in 1997 and 1998, the Internal Revenue Code treats the probate estate and the trust estate similarly.

Marital Rights

Sometimes living trusts are suggested as a way to avoid a spouse's rights. Under Florida law, a surviving spouse unhappy with a will is entitled to take as an alternative approximately 30% of the estate. This is true unless the parties have entered into a valid prenuptial or postnuptial agreement. However, the protective provisions giving the surviving spouse 30% of the assets passing under a will do not seem to apply to living trusts. A spouse, either through anger or misunderstanding or some other human frailty, may make provisions in a living trust that are extremely difficult for the surviving spouse to swallow. Because there is no protection under Florida law for the surviving spouse when it comes to living trusts, the surviving spouse may find himself or herself in a very bad situation—even disinherited. This has been the subject of much discussion, and a change making living trusts and wills the same for marital rights is anticipated.

Will Contests

Sometimes living trusts are suggested as a way to avoid will contests.

Technically, of course, this is correct, because if there is a living trust, most of the assets will not be passing under the will; they will be passing under the trust. If they are under the trust, then the contest would not be a will contest—it would be a trust contest. Also, any person who has an interest in the trust, either claimed or real, can contest the trust up until the time the assets are distributed. Under a will, the period during which there could be a will contest by heirs or beneficiaries is limited. With a trust, this period remains open.

Deeding Real Estate into a Living Trust

Any deed which is effective to transfer real property to another person can effectively transfer real property to your trustee and into your trust. Legally, the transfer of title to your trustee gives the trustee every power over the property that is granted in the trust agreement. Very few people know what your trust agreement says, so most people don't know what authority your trustee has.

If the issue doesn't arise sooner, verification of the trustee's authority ordinarily will be required when the property is sold. Before insuring that the buyer is receiving good title to the property, the title insurance issuer will want assurances that the trustee has the power under the trust agreement to sell the property. If a typical real estate deed was used to transfer property to the trust, the only document that contains all the powers of the trustee is the trust agreement. It is likely that the title insurance issuer will require that the entire trust agreement, or at least substantial parts of it, be recorded so that the powers of the trustee are in the public records.

To avoid making public a document intended to remain private, many careful attorneys use a special deed that recites the authority of the trustee. In fact, many attorneys will take an additional precaution. They provide for a successor trustee in the trust agreement and include the name of that successor trustee in the deed. If the current trustee has died or resigned when it is time to convey the property, and if the successor is acting as trustee, there is no need to examine and record the trust agreement to confirm the trustee's identity.

Some people do not object to having their living trusts recorded, but most do. When a trust is recorded, it becomes part of the public record. Anyone can read the document and see who is to receive what property.

Of course, if the property you want to transfer to your trust is homestead, there are further complications. (See Chapter 6 for a discussion of homestead property.)

Privacy

Privacy is always an important issue. With a trust, there is a loss of privacy while you're alive, with a will, a loss of privacy after your death. The will is recorded after death and is therefore open to all persons. Conversely, the trust frequently must be shown to persons while you are alive. It is unlikely that stock transfer agents will transfer assets into or out of the trust without being given the opportunity to photocopy the trust. Because of this, there is a loss of privacy while you're alive because the trust must be shown to persons in order to have them recognize the validity of the trust. One argument occasionally made for trusts by people who do not know better is that your assets passing under a will are open to inspection by anyone wanting to find out "what you were worth." This is not true. Under a will, inventories listing all assets passing through the will are required to be filed with the probate court. However, these inventories are sealed by the court and are not available to the public.

Is a Living Trust Right for You?

Frequently it is, but many times it may not be. When all assets are held jointly, the living trust will not save probate costs, since there is no probate. Rather than doing two trusts while both spouses are alive, it may be cheaper and wiser to do just one trust later when there is just one spouse and the property is no longer jointly held. However, if there is concern that one of the parties will be incapacitated or unable to manage the assets at that time, it may be wisest to do the living trust for both the husband and wife when the estate planning is being done.

Revocable trusts have an advantage over wills in their flexibility over who the trustee *can* be. Under Florida law, it is necessary that the executor or personal representative of the estate be either a blood relative or the spouse of a blood relative, a resident of the state of Florida, or a trust company authorized to do business in Florida. This is typical in many states and, in fact, Florida grants more latitude than many. However, the trustee may be any individual or trust company. Generally speaking, the older a person is, the more important and beneficial the living trust becomes. The reason is that as a person grows older, the chances of being incapacitated increase. This time of incapacity is when the trust benefits arise. Younger persons are less likely to be incapacitated and to realize the benefits of a living trust.

The size of the assets in the estate also helps in determining whether a living trust will be useful. Persons with quite modest estates may feel that they do not want the expense of a living trust. Conversely, persons with very large estates frequently choose not to set up a living trust because the expenses of settling their estate are frequently the same whether the assets are passing under a will or under a trust. In some instances, these people will be able to save money by having their assets pass under a will instead of a trust. A slight estate tax benefit can arise with a will because it is usually easier to support deductions on a federal estate tax return for the personal representative's fees than it is to support deductions on the estate tax return in the same amount for trustee's fees. Persons with medium to medium-large estates generally will see some benefits in having a living trust. A broad generalization, and one subject of debate, is that people with an estate of several hundred thousand dollars or less usually benefit less from living trusts. Persons with assets over this amount probably should consider the merits of a living trust. In any case, if you are discussing the advisability of a living trust with your attorney, talk about the pros and cons noted in this chapter. Your attorney may have some additional suggestions or comments.

Inter vivos trusts can be extremely useful for some estates. They are essential tools in estate planning, particularly if you're concerned about loss of ability to manage assets in the future. They provide privacy after death and frequently save money on moderate-sized estates. While *inter vivos* trusts frequently cost two to three times more than a will to set up, they usually make up this difference in savings of administration costs after your death.

6

HOMESTEAD

Homestead property rights were introduced into Florida law in the state constitution of 1868. These provisions were intended to secure the family home—or, as was more usual in 1868, the family farm—to prevent the family from becoming destitute. Under Florida law, the homestead is protected in several ways. Under the homestead real estate tax exemption, part of the assessed value of the homestead is exempted from real estate taxation. The homestead exemption from forced sale means creditors cannot require the homestead be sold for debts, other than for taxes, assessments, or certain other debts directly related to the property. There are restrictions placed on the owner's ability to transfer the homestead, both during life and at death. The laws regulating the transfer of the homestead at death are of particular concern to the estate planner and are the subject of this chapter.

Clarifying which homestead provisions are being discussed is important. All these laws purport to regulate property which is labeled as "homestead." It is reasonable, but also incorrect, to assume that the meaning of the term "homestead" is clear and consistent. Unfortunately, that is not the case. In Florida, your residence may be your homestead for one purpose and not for another. The conditions vary that determine whether any specific property qualifies as a homestead and, if so, is subject to a specific homestead provision. This is one reason that homestead is one of the most confusing areas of Florida law, and indeed that the term "homestead" has earned the nickname "the legal chameleon."

Despite the complexities of homestead law, it is important to be aware of the basic concepts when structuring your estate plan. These laws affect whether you can transfer your home during life or after death, who can inherit it, and under what conditions. Lifetime transfers are only restricted when the homeowner is married. A married owner of a homestead can mortgage, sell, or give away the homestead only if his or her spouse consents and joins in the transfer. Transfers at death are restricted if the homeowner is married or has a child under the age of 18 (a minor). Let's take a closer look at the homestead laws that restrict the transfer of your Florida home at your death.

Homestead—What Is It?

Generally, if you live in Florida in a home you own, that home (including a condominium) is your homestead. Laws restricting the transfer of a homestead apply automatically to every Florida residence that fits the description of homestead. There is no easy way to opt out and avoid the homestead laws which dictate who may inherit the homestead.

The property cannot exceed 160 acres outside city limits or one-half acre within city limits. If you transfer your home into your living trust (a subject we'll discuss in more detail later in this chapter), it's still your homestead. If you and your spouse own your home jointly, it is not a homestead.

There are a few more legal terms we need to review before we can talk about homestead transfer restrictions.

Lineal Descendants, Per Stirpes

The law often requires that your homestead be inherited by your "lineal descendants, per stirpes." Lineal descendants are your children, grandchildren, great grandchildren, and so on down the line of your direct descendants. We talked about the meaning of "per stirpes" in Chapter 2, but it isn't an easy term to remember. When property is inherited by your lineal descendants, per stirpes, there will be one share for each of your children who is living and one share for any child who is deceased but who has a living lineal descendant. The deceased child's share will be shared equally among his or her children.

Devise

A "devise" is a gift of real property by your will. "Devise" is also a verb which means to give away property by your will. Under certain circumstances the owner of a homestead is not allowed to devise the homestead. Instead, the homestead must be inherited by specified family members.

Intestate

If you die without a valid will, you die "intestate." Special intestacy laws enacted by the Florida legislature become, in effect, your will and determine who inherits your property. Even if you have a valid will but you own property which is not validly devised by your will, that property passes under these intestacy laws.

Who Gets Your Homestead When You Die?

Homestead restrictions do not apply to your Florida residence in two cases: Joint Tenancy with Right of Survivorship or Tenants by the Entirety.

As noted above, if your residence is owned by you and your spouse jointly, it is not "homestead" under the laws restricting the transfer of homestead and is not subject to any homestead transfer restrictions at your death. The survivorship provision takes precedence. At the death of one spouse, the residence becomes the sole property of the surviving spouse.

No Surviving Spouse and No Minor Children

If you are not married and your children are adults, you can give your home to anyone in your will. If you have a minor child, you are not permitted under Florida law to will your home to *anyone at all.* If you have a spouse but do not have a minor child, you may devise your homestead *only* to your spouse.

What happens to your homestead when you are not allowed to devise it? Your surviving spouse receives a life estate (i.e., the right to live in the house rent-free for your spouse's lifetime). Your lineal descendants who are alive at the time of your death own a remainder interest, which means they will share full ownership of the homestead at the time of your spouse's death. This arrangement is almost always a bad one. Your minor children will have a legal ownership in your home. Selling the home will be full of legal complications because of the minor children's ownership. Talk with your attorney about potential problems and possible alternatives.

At this point, a review of these homestead laws from another angle may be helpful. Let's look at the variety of situations which can arise and see how the restrictions apply in each case.

Restrictions

If you have a valid will, you may (or may not) devise your homestead in accordance with the following rules:

Surviving Spouse and Minor Child

If you are survived by a spouse and at least one minor child, the homestead cannot be devised to anyone, not even your spouse, under any circumstances. Any attempt to devise your home in your will is invalid. It must pass under the intestacy laws. Your surviving spouse is given the homestead for life, and your lineal descendants who are living at the time of your death will share ownership of the homestead.

Surviving Spouse and No Minor Child

The homestead can only be devised to your spouse, and your spouse must receive complete ownership. No restrictions may be imposed, such as limiting ownership to twenty years, or life, or even just a one-half interest. Any devise other than a devise of full ownership to your spouse is invalid and the homestead will given to your spouse and your lineal descendants under the intestacy laws.

No Surviving Spouse and Minor Child

If you are unmarried but have a child under the age of 18 at the time of your death, you may not devise your home to anyone. Any provision in your will attempting to give your property to anyone is invalid. Your home will pass to all your lineal descendants.

No Surviving Spouse and No Minor Child

You may devise your homestead to anyone you wish. It is not subject to homestead transfer restrictions.

Waiver of Homestead Provisions

The rules limiting your ability to devise your homestead or otherwise restricting who may inherit this property are intended to protect your spouse and your minor children. A child is not allowed to give up a legal right; however, it is possible for a spouse to waive his or her rights.

Waiving a spouse's constitutional protection of the homestead can be done before marriage, after marriage, or after the death of the owner of the property. If it is done before marriage, the document is called a prenuptial agreement. If it is waived during the marriage, a postnuptial agreement must be used. This document is subject to stricter requirements than the prenuptial agreement (see Chapter 13). After the death of the property owner, the surviving spouse may decline to accept the homestead and the property would pass as if the spouse were dead. Declining to accept the homestead after a death is called a disclaimer.

Waivers as They Affect Lineal Descendants

Betsy and Tom are both widowed with adult children. They plan to be married and live in Betsy's home. Before the wedding, they sign prenuptial agreements giving up all rights in each other's separate property, specifically including Tom's homestead rights in Betsy's homestead. Betsy's will instructs her personal representative to sell her homestead and donate the proceeds to her church. When Betsy dies, what happens to her home? Until recently, Florida courts did not agree on the effect of Tom's waiver.

One Florida court said that because Tom waived his rights in Betsy's homestead, he should be treated as if he were dead for purposes of the homestead laws. If so, Betsy had no spouse and no minor child. She could devise her homestead to anyone. The church receives the proceeds of the sale.

Another Florida court insisted that the law should continue to recognize that Betsy was married. She could only devise her home to Tom. The devise to the church is invalid. The homestead is inherited under the law which gave Tom a life estate in the home and Betsy's children ownership of the home following Tom's death. Tom has waived his rights to the homestead; therefore, Betsy's children own the homestead at Betsy's death.

The Florida Supreme Court has now ruled that if a spouse waives his or her rights in homestead, that spouse will be treated as dead for purposes of the homestead rules. If the homestead owner has no minor children, there is no family member whom the homestead laws are intended to protect and the homestead may be devised to anyone. The effect of this decision is that a waiver signed by the surviving spouse is effective as to both the surviving spouse and any adult children. The property is no longer required to be inherited by the owner's lineal descendants. Of course, if there is a minor child, the constitutional protections are still effective and the property goes to all lineal descendants.

Homestead and Revocable Trusts

If you establish a trust during your life, it is an *inter vivos* trust. (A trust which is provided for in your will and goes into effect after your death is a testamentary trust.) If you are able to cancel the trust at any time, it is a revocable *inter vivos* trust. The most common form of revocable *inter vivos* trust is commonly known as a living trust. Living trusts are fully discussed in Chapter 5.

A large number of Floridians own their own homes, and a rapidly growing number of Floridians are establishing living trusts. Many homeowners who have living trusts have transferred all their property, including their homesteads, into their trusts, usually in an attempt to avoid probate. This is a mistake because homestead is not a probate asset and does not go through probate. Further, the resulting interaction of homestead laws and trust laws has caused considerable confusion and some disagreement among judges, attorneys, laypersons, and title companies.

Homestead Property in Your Living Trust

One significant point is clear. Putting the homestead real estate in a living trust does not prevent the application of homestead restrictions on transfer. The property is still a homestead and is still subject to the laws concerning homestead property.

The validity of transferring your homestead into a trust during your life is open to significant challenge. Major title companies insuring Florida real estate are issuing cautionary notices warning of the dangers of transferring a Floridian's homestead into a living trust. If you transfer property to yourself as trustee of a typical living trust, several title insurance companies are now requiring that, before insuring title to a purchaser of the property, several things must happen. First, you, as the trustee, must transfer the property as if the property were in the trust by signing a trustee's deed. Secondly, the title company requires satisfactory proof that you were not survived by a spouse or minor child. If you have a spouse or minor child, then the transfer of your homestead may be invalid and court procedures to clear title may be necessary.

Summary

Because of the uncertainties surrounding homestead, it is a good idea for a husband and wife in a stable marriage of some duration to hold the property as tenants by the entirety or as joint tenants with right of survivorship (see Chapter 7 for definitions of these terms). Homestead, generally speaking, should not be placed in a revocable, *inter vivos* trust. Particularly, don't place the homestead in a living trust in order to avoid probate. Many of the major title insurance companies are requiring that there be a full probate even if the property is in a trust. It is better to have the property owned jointly, or if not jointly, then individually.

In this chapter, you will learn:

- what "joint tenancy/right of survivorship" means
- how it is different from "tenancy in common"
- what "tenancy by the entirety" means
- which states are community property states
- how gift taxes are affected when a joint tenancy is created
- what happens when joint accounts are terminated
- what to do upon the death of a cotenant
- what property should be held jointly
- whether or not the marital home should be jointly owned
- how the estate tax is apportioned
- how joint safe deposit boxes are handled after death
- how you can have too much joint property

7

JOINT PROPERTY

Joint property simply means that more than one person owns the same property at the same time. There can be co-ownership of any type of property: real property (real estate), tangible personal property (such as cars, paintings, and jewelry), or intangible personal property (such as stocks and bonds).

Joint ownership comes in two general types. One automatically passes to the surviving persons in the event of the death of one of the people whose names appeared as co-owners of the joint property. This is called joint tenancy with right of survivorship. In the other type of joint ownership, when one of the owners dies, the property does not pass to the surviving joint owners. This is called tenancy in common. The deceased owner's share of the joint property passes to the beneficiary named in his or her will or trust or, if none, under the intestacy (no will) laws of Florida. Joint ownership of property is used by estate planners because it offers many advantages. However, as we will discuss later, it can create problems and certainly is not a substitute for a will.

Joint Tenancy with Right of Survivorship

A joint tenancy with right of survivorship means that property is owned by two or more persons and that when one person dies, his or her interest will pass to the remaining co-owner. (For simplicity's sake, we will assume that only two people hold the joint property.) If one person dies, the property then passes outright to the surviving co-owner (or cotenant, as the attorney frequently calls a joint owner). It passes free of any probate and need not have been in any type of trust. Passing free of any probate offers advantages.

When creating a joint tenancy, it is always desirable and many times necessary to provide in the documents setting up the ownership that the joint tenancy is with right of survivorship. Failure to include the words *"with right of survivorship"* or similar words may mean the property will become a tenancy in common.

Tenancy in Common

A tenancy in common differs from a joint tenancy with right of survivorship in that the interest of a deceased owner in a tenancy in common *does not pass* on death to the co-owner. The interest of the cotenant or co-owner in property held as a tenancy in common passes to whomever the deceased co-owner has directed in his or her will. What this means is that property held in the tenancy in common usually passes through probate and will wind up in the hands of the heirs or beneficiaries of the deceased.

Tenancies in common are frequently used when people purchase property for a business purpose, combining their capital and time or talents. The owner does not wish his or her interest to go to the other owner on death, but rather to his or her beneficiaries such as a spouse, children, or other family members. Tenancy in common, therefore, is more frequently seen in business ventures. Sometimes it is used for estate planning purposes when the intent is to pass the ownership in a specialized fashion not to the co-owner.

Tenancy by the Entirety

A special type of joint property with right of survivorship is called a tenancy by the entirety. "Entirety" comes from the concept in early English law that a husband and a wife were one. The two married people made up one entire person, "an entirety"; therefore, a tenancy by the entirety can never be between persons who are not married to each other. There will always be one man and one woman, and never more than two people, in a tenancy by the entirety. Florida automatically provides for survivorship with a tenancy by the entirety. If you own property in a tenancy by the entirety, your spouse will always inherit this property if he or she survives. Under Florida law, a tenancy by the entirety *automatically* arises when a husband and wife take title to real estate as husband and wife. Therefore, if the deed to your home says "to John Jones and Mary Jones, husband and wife," this automatically, under Florida law, creates a tenancy by the entirety because the parties have been identified as being husband and wife on the deed. The real estate will pass to the surviving spouse on the death of the other.

This is not the case, however, in tangible personal property such as paintings, automobiles, and other possessions. If you want these items in a tenancy by the entirety, you must spell this out. Since a tenancy by the entirety operates very much like a joint tenancy with right of survivorship, most people make the tangible personal property a joint tenancy with right of survivorship. There is no probate and very little red tape. Types of property such as homes, which are essential to the operating of the family unit, are usually joint tenancy with right of survivorship or are a tenancy by the entirety.

There is no difference between tenancy by the entirety and joint tenancy with right of survivorship between spouses when it comes to the question of who will inherit the property if one of the spouses dies. The answer will always be the same for either of the two tenancies: the surviving spouse will inherit. If your deed to the home provides tenancy with right of survivorship instead of husband and wife, or husband and wife as a tenancy by the entirety, do not fear; this still means that the property will pass to the surviving spouse if either of you dies.

Community Property

Community property is a concept which comes to us not from the law of England where most of our legal heritage arose, but from what is known as civil law. Civil law developed from Roman laws, was incorporated into the laws of France and Spain, and came to the United States with persons from those countries. One state, Louisiana, was founded by French émigrés, and seven states have a strong Spanish heritage: Arizona, California, Idaho, Nevada, New Mexico, Texas, and Washington. These states are community property states.

Community property is property acquired during marriage through means other than gift or inheritance. The concept is confusing to many people because of the power of community property law to change the ownership of property even though the title to the property reads in a different way. For example, in California community property in the form of stocks and bonds may be in the name of just the husband or just the wife. Nevertheless, even though the title may be in just one spouse's name, because it is community property, the other spouse automatically has a one-half interest in the property.

Suppose the couple moves from California to Florida. The title doesn't change. The property is still in the name of the husband only, but the owners of the property are still the husband *and* wife. Under community property law, the actual ownership did not change when the couple crossed the Florida state line. It remains community property no matter where they move. If you have been a resident of Louisiana or one of the Spanish-heritage states named above, and were married at the time you lived in that state, you probably have community property even though you now live in Florida.

What Is Community Property?

Earnings made while living in a community property state are community property. Property purchased with community property is community property. Note that if community property earnings from California are used to purchase a lot in Florida, the real estate investment may be titled in one person's name, but it is in fact community property owned equally by the two persons. As a rule of thumb (and only that), property acquired before marriage or before living in a community property state is usually not considered to be community property. The same holds for property acquired during marriage while living in a community property state if the property was acquired by gift or inheritance. Property in the form of compensation for a personal injury is generally considered to be the property of the individual who was injured, and in most instances it is not community property.

People coming to Florida from Puerto Rico, or from any Hispanic country, should note that their property *may be* community property. Puerto Rico, with its Spanish heritage, shares the community property concept with the Western states mentioned earlier.

Ending Community Property

Florida provides that people may sever, divide up, or "erase" community property aspects when they come to Florida. Each person can sign a document stipulating that whatever community property they had is now divided in whatever fashion they agree upon. A lawyer doing the estate plan in Florida can look at the title to the property and know for certain who the owner is. If it were still community property, one person's name might be on the title, but the ownership might be equally divided between the two persons, causing confusion and perhaps undesirable results in the estate plan. However, splitting up community property can have some disadvantages from a tax point of view.

Gifting Joint Property

We have talked about general types of property co-ownership: joint property with right of survivorship, tenancies in common, and tenancies by the entirety, as well as the peculiar species of co-ownership known as community property. With these basic building blocks in place, let's take a look at some of the gift tax aspects and estate tax aspects of joint ownership property. We'll discuss the advantages, disadvantages, some pitfalls, and some of the unusual benefits that can arise through the proper use of joint property.

Gift Taxes When a Joint Tenancy Is Created

When a joint tenancy is created between a husband and wife, there is no gift tax. A husband and wife can make gifts to each other free of any gift tax. When a joint tenancy with right of survivorship (more easily referred to as a joint tenancy) is created between people not married to each other, the question of whether there is a gift depends upon the contribution of each of the parties. If each of the parties contributes equal amounts, neither has more than the other and there is no gift. When one person contributes more than the other, a gift is created and a gift tax liability arises. However, there are exceptions in the case of US savings bonds, joint brokerage accounts, and joint bank accounts. Here, the gift is considered made not when the joint tenancy is *created*, but when assets in excess of what one person contributed are taken out. Thus, if two people have a joint bank account—say a mother and a son—and the mother puts in all the money, there is no gift until the son takes money out. US savings bonds, joint brokerage accounts, and joint bank accounts are exceptions to the general rule that in a joint tenancy a gift will arise when one puts in more than the other.

In the case of joint property, income tax rules are similar to the gift tax in that each joint tenant must report his or her share of the income on his or her own separate tax return. Again, however, note the exception when it comes to a joint bank account. In this case, all the income from the account is reported to the social security number of the sole contributor to the bank account, and this person reports all the income on his or her income tax return. This is true even though another person's name may be on the account as a joint tenant. Remember, there is no gift on a joint bank account until one of the people takes out more than he or she contributed. The situation is similar with joint brokerage accounts and United States bonds.

In joint property (other than United States savings bonds, joint accounts, and certain types of brokerage accounts), the income is considered to be owned equally by all persons on the account. Income tax savings through the use of joint tenancies are usually nominal. After all, most husbands and wives file joint tax returns. Other co-owners are likely to be in the same income tax bracket. In the case of children, because of the kiddie tax it is not possible to effect significant income tax savings if the child is under age 14.

The "kiddie tax" is a provision in the income tax law which says that children under the age of 14 who have income (such as interest on bank accounts) must pay income tax at the parent's income tax bracket. The parents and the young child must pay at the same income tax rate so there is no tax savings.

Termination of Joint Accounts

Joint accounts with right of survivorship and tenancies in common can be terminated at will. All that is necessary for one of the parties to terminate the account is to take the money out. It can be done unilaterally without the consent of the other or others.

This is not the case, however, in a tenancy by the entirety. A tenancy by the entirety can be terminated only by mutual consent of the husband and wife. It would be terminated by a divorce decree. Just as there was no gift tax when the joint account was created between the husband and wife, so there is no gift tax when the joint account between husband and wife or the tenancy by the entirety is terminated.

Income Tax on Termination of a Joint Tenancy

Just as the income followed the ownership of the joint tenancy, so the income tax consequences on termination follow the joint tenancy. If one co-owner in a bank account has been reporting all the income, he or she will be subject to any income tax consequence on termination.

On the other hand, if the ownership is of improved real estate, the question becomes more complicated. If the joint tenancy is being terminated because the property is being sold, then the gain or loss will be reported to the person based on his or her fractional interest in the property. This will be adjusted for depreciation and other adjustments that naturally occur when improved real property for investment purposes is sold. If the property was inherited, the basis will be the date-of-death value plus any cash contributions for improvement made by the cotenants (co-owners), less depreciation. Let's look at some of the tax consequences on death and see how joint tenancies are treated for estate tax purposes. The results in some instances can be surprising.

Death of a Cotenant

If a cotenant of a joint tenancy dies and the cotenancy is a tenancy with right of survivorship or tenancy by the entirety, all the property goes to the surviving cotenant. In the case of a tenancy by the entirety, there is no estate tax because of the tax-free right to transfer property on death between a husband and wife (unless the spouse is not a US citizen). If the parties are not married to each other, then the deceased cotenant will be considered, for federal and Florida estate tax purposes, to have transferred the value of his or her interest to the surviving tenant.

What About a Joint Bank Account?

If the cotenant furnished all the money in a joint bank account, there would be no gift made when the joint tenancy was created because of the exception for such accounts. The deceased, for tax purposes, would be considered the sole owner of the joint bank account. The full amount of the joint bank account would be in his or her estate and the full value of the joint bank account would be taxed in that estate.

The obligation to pay estate taxes will be governed by the will of the person who died. Frequently, the will has a provision that all estate taxes should be paid from the residue of the estate. That is to say, the money passing under the will or trust will pay the tax, and not the joint property. The estate taxes are actually being paid by the beneficiaries of the residue of the estate, who may or may not be beneficiaries of the joint account. Someone is going to wind up paying someone else's tax bill.

Uses of Joint Property

Thus far, we have talked about the types of tenancies, their creation, their termination while the parties are still alive, and their termination on the death of the parties. Now it is time to think about some of the uses of these tenancies, to develop some general rules, and to compare and contrast joint tenancies with solely owned property.

What Property Should Be Held Jointly?

It is a good idea for married people to have a joint checking account, perhaps a joint savings account, and the homestead held in both names. The reason for having checking and savings accounts in both names is having ready funds available in case one of the spouses dies. It can be a source of comfort for the surviving spouse to know that he or she can continue writing checks or drawing funds and have a ready source of cash.

Also, from a practical standpoint, there are expenses associated with death. It is sometimes necessary to advance funds to buy airplane tickets for children or relatives, pay funeral bills, and perhaps pay medical bills. Having a joint account the surviving spouse can immediately draw upon can be a real benefit, both psychologically and financially.

The Marital Home

When it comes to the house, opinions differ, but in a stable, long-term marital relationship, having the house owned jointly is a good idea. If the house is in just one person's name and that person dies, the house probably will be homestead under Florida law. If it is homestead, it will pass to the surviving spouse unless there are minor children. If there are minor children, this will cause a guardianship for the minors and this involves courts, lawyers, and red tape. If the property is held jointly, the surviving spouse can feel more securely that *"This is my home."*

If the property is not willed to the surviving spouse and is not joint property, and if there are any minor children, the Florida homestead law will apply. The Florida homestead law provides a life estate to the surviving spouse with the remainder in the children. This usually is not a good result. After all, if you want to sell your house, should you have to ask your children if you can do so? When you sell it, what do you get? The surviving spouse only gets the value of the life estate, not the full ownership. This is not a good result unless it is done deliberately because of tax considerations or because of a second marriage.

To be sure, there are arguments, including income tax considerations, that sometimes suggest that the property should not be held jointly. If jointly owned, there is only an increase in tax basis to one-half of fair market value on date of death and one-half of basis prior to death. But on the other hand, there is also the $250,000 capital gain exclusion for the sale of your residence exclusion and, as noted, we are dealing with general rules. It usually is best to have the house jointly held. It meets many emotional needs. It facilitates the administration of the property. It causes no estate tax to arise, and the income tax problems, if any, are nominal. It avoids the problems of homestead, since joint property takes precedence over the homestead law. Joint spousal ownership of the house usually makes things easier for all concerned.

If the parties are not married to each other, the question of what should be held as joint tenancy with right of survivorship can be answered very simply. What do you want to pass to this person if you die? If you want your interest to go to that person and you trust him or her completely, by all means, have it as joint tenancy with right of survivorship. This is simple, clean, quick, and clear. On the other hand, if you want your interest to pass to your beneficiaries under your will, then do not have it as joint tenancy with right of survivorship. Hold the property in a tenancy in common. More than one person's estate plan has been frustrated because "someone" decided to have the property held as joint tenants with right of survivorship when what was really intended was a tenancy in common—or because "someone" decided that the property should be held jointly to avoid probate. Do not let other people make the decision as to how the title is to be held for you. Look at titles to property, real estate, stocks, and bank accounts. If a title is held jointly, ask yourself, "Is this where I want this property to go?"

Estate Tax Apportionment

There is another significant question when you are considering whether to have property owned jointly: "Are there any estate taxes to be paid?" If the answer is yes, be sure to ask who should pay the estate tax on this property. In the case of small joint accounts with right of survivorship—perhaps that of a grandmother with a grandson's name on it or a parent with a child's name on it—it may be a perfectly good result that there should be no taxes charged to that joint account. What is intended is a ready source of funds. Any taxes that might arise can be paid from the residue of the property under the will.

On the other hand, if there will be estate taxes, if the value of the joint account is significant, and if the person whose name appears on the joint account is not the sole beneficiary of your estate plan, there may be a problem. It may not be entirely clear to everyone why one child is to inherit a substantial amount of money from the joint account, yet the estate taxes on the joint asset are paid by all the children from the residue of the estate.

Champ has three daughters: two daughters live outside Florida, and one, Harriet, lives nearby. Champ decides it "would be nice" if Harriet's name were on the joint account. A substantial bank account which Champ owns is made joint with Harriet. On Champ's death, Harriet inherits the money by right of survivorship per the account contract. However, Champ's will says that all estate taxes shall be paid from the residue of his estate passing under his will. Therefore, all three children must share equally in paying the estate taxes since the taxes come out of the residue of Champ's will that is divided among all three children. Harriet, in effect, will benefit by having the other two daughters pay two-thirds of the estate tax on the money which she inherits in the joint account. The other daughters are already miffed by the fact that Harriet is inheriting this money that they feel should belong to them equally. When they find out they also have to pay estate tax on this money that Harriet is inheriting, they are going to call their lawyers.

The clause in the will which says that all estate taxes are paid from the residue of the estate may need to be changed. Since the children are the beneficiaries of the residue of the estate, they are paying the tax for this other child. Is this the correct result? The answer probably is no. This type of problem occurs frequently. The solution is to say in Champ's will that he intends the joint account to pass to Harriet free of any estate taxes being paid by Harriet, or to say that estate taxes are to be charged to the account also.

Totten Trust

There is a peculiar type of ownership that really isn't joint property. It isn't a trust. In fact, it is hard to legally pigeonhole exactly what it is. The name of this strange type of ownership is a Totten trust. ("Totten" comes from the name of the people who first created this type of account.) Actually, it really is not a trust at all. A Totten trust is a type of account typically found in a bank which identifies a particular individual as the owner of the account; after this individual's name, the words "in trust for" appear. A similar account is available in some stock brokerage firms and is known as a "Pay on Death" or a P.O.D. account.

These accounts function in an interesting and very useful way. While the person who created the account is still alive, that person can add funds to the trust or take them out. No questions asked. No restrictions. No problems. Upon the death of the creator of the account, the person whose name appears after the phrase "in trust for" or "P.O.D." can take the funds in the account with no questions asked as long as he or she provides a death certificate showing that the person who created the account is deceased. These types of accounts are favored when a person wants a moderate amount of money to go to a particular individual.

The assets in the account do not go through probate, although certainly they are still subject to federal and Florida estate tax. No gift tax arose because the person who created the account could take out the money as long as he or she was alive. Thus there was no completed gift.

These accounts are frequently used by grandparents who want to provide "a little bit of money" for their grandchildren. A grandmother can set up an account in her name and a grandchild's name. If the grandmother needs the money, she can always take it out. On the other hand, if she does not take it out, then the money will pass to the grandchild with no strings attached. It is not uncommon for one person to have a number of these accounts, each with a different grandchild's name on it.

Sometimes a child's name will be put on the account, although frequently accounts with the child's name on them are held with joint tenancy with right of survivorship. Remember, with a joint tenancy with the right of survivorship, the child can take the money out if necessary to help out the parent if the parent is incapacitated and cannot sign. With the Totten trust or P.O.D. account, no one can take the money out until the creator is deceased.

Joint Safe Deposit Boxes

If a safe deposit box is jointly held, whether between a husband and wife or other parties, the *box* is jointly held but the *contents* are not. Ownership of the contents is dependent upon how the contents are titled. All that is jointly held is the box itself. Making the box jointly owned does not in some magical way transform the contents from solely owned to jointly owned.

Too Much Joint Property

There can be too much joint property. Not infrequently, people say, "Make everything joint; avoid probate. You don't need a will and you don't have to worry about anything." Common sense tells us that nothing can be that simple.

Let us look at a problem that occurs with too much joint property. Jim and Karen have been married to each other for many years. Their financial adviser tells them that they should have wills and do some estate planning. On the other hand, their neighbors, Hugh and Charlotte, say "That's crazy. You don't need to spend that kind of money. All you need to do is have everything joint." So Jim and Karen make everything joint. They save a lot of money—probably $500 or $600 in estate planning fees.

Jim dies and now Karen owns everything. Karen dies and the children look to see what they have to do in order to pay any estate taxes due and divide up the property. They find they owe the federal government $233,000 in estate taxes! It turns out that after Jim's death, Karen did a simple will giving everything to them equally. With Jim's IRA that she inherited, his life insurance, their home, and the money they accumulated, the property he had left her had grown to $1,400,000 by the time Karen died.

The trap of joint property has been sprung! The government is the beneficiary, and the children are the losers. This could have been avoided if Jim and Karen had set up a *marital deduction residuary* type of estate plan. No matter who died first, the exempt amount of $625,000 in 1998 (and increasing as discussed in Chapter 8) of that total property would have gone into a trust. That trust would have been for the surviving spouse. In fact, the surviving spouse could have been the trustee. Under the terms of that trust, all the income would have been paid to the surviving spouse. In fact, principal could have been available to the surviving spouse if necessary for health and maintenance. When the surviving spouse died, that trust could then have had all the property distributed to the kids—tax free. The inheritance could have passed tax-free at the death of the first spouse and at the time of the death of the second spouse. When Karen died, the exempt amount from Jim would have been sheltered together with all the appreciation that occurred thereafter. Karen's death would not have caused any taxes to arise because her estate would have been under the exempt amount. We will talk more about this type of trust in Chapter 12.

Jim and Karen did save a little money by making everything joint but not much, especially when you consider the $233,000 in taxes. This simple mistake is repeated again and again in Florida. You *can* have too much joint property. This is possible because of the tax law which says that on the death of the surviving spouse, the federal government will tax everything over the exempt amount. Be sure you use the exempt amount (also known as the equivalent exemption) on the death of the first spouse if there is any possibility that on the death of the surviving spouse, the estate could *ever* exceed the exempt amount. If you add up everything you own and then factor in inflation, it is surprising how often the surviving spouse's estate could exceed the exempt amount. Because of the high rate of estate tax, be sure you don't walk away from that deduction that the first spouse has. The deduction can be used through a trust created in a will (a testamentary trust) or in a trust created during a lifetime (a living trust).

Frequently, there will be other considerations. When Bill and Vivian discussed this with their estate planner, they looked at each other and said frankly, "We worked for this property. We have been a partnership. The kids can be glad they're getting anything. Let them pay the tax. We made the money in the United States, and we'll pay the tax gladly." This is a conversation repeated many times, but many more times people say, "What? You mean to tell me by having everything joint that my kids are going to have to pay an extra $233,000 in estate taxes? No way."

In this chapter, you will learn:

- about the Revolution of 1976
- the definition of a gift
- who pays the gift tax
- about the annual exclusion
- the equivalent exemption or equivalent deduction
- gift tax deduction
- Florida gift and estate taxes
- medical and tuition exclusion
- gifts with a spouse
- making gifts today
- when a gift is a gift, with no strings attached

8

GIFT TAXES IN A NUTSHELL

Most people are aware that there is a federal estate tax; fewer people know that there is a federal gift tax; and almost no one, except tax professionals, understands much about either of them or the way they interact with each other and with the Florida estate tax.

The good news is that Florida has no gift tax, and Florida's estate tax doesn't cost you anything. The bad news is that Uncle Sam has both a gift tax and an estate tax, with lots of complicated rules and tables for figuring who owes what and when.

The Revolution of 1976

In 1976, a revolution occurred in estate planning. The tax reform act adopted that year completely changed the taxation of gifts and estates. Previously, each individual, during his or her lifetime, could make gifts totaling not more than $30,000 without being subject to any gift tax liability. Additionally, each individual could make gifts totaling not more than $3,000 each calendar year to an unlimited number of recipients. The estate tax laws permitted only $60,000 of assets to be given away at death free of estate tax. Because the gift tax rate was lower than the estate tax rate, it was more advantageous from a tax standpoint to make lifetime gifts than it was to pass property on death. Since 1976, there is no difference in tax rates. A uniform transfer tax ended the favorable tax treatment for gifts. In fact, the gift tax and estate tax are frequently referred to together as the transfer tax.

What Is a Gift?

Let's look at what is included in the term "gift," in terms of gift tax. Any time a person makes a transfer to another person without receiving full value for the transfer, the Internal Revenue Service considers that a gift has been made. This statement may not be perfectly accurate in some unusual circumstances, but it serves as a good statement of the philosophy governing the question of whether a person has made a gift or not. The obvious examples of gifts of money, stocks, or real estate are easy, but people make much more complex gifts, and sometimes are not even aware that they have made a gift.

Sometimes the opening of a joint account can be a gift. Usually, however, this is not a gift until someone actually takes the money out of the joint account. While this may be the rule for joint bank accounts, a different rule applies if a person has real estate deeded to himself or herself and another person. Having the other person's name appear on the deed is a gift. Sometimes it is never intended to be a gift. It is intended to be a matter of convenience. The thinking may be "I want him or her to have this when I pass on." Nevertheless, placing another person's name on a deed with your own is going to be viewed by the Internal Revenue Service as a gift.

Who Pays the Gift Tax?

It is important to note that when a person receives a gift, he or she usually does not have to pay the gift tax. The transfer (gift) tax is charged to the giver of the gift, not the receiver of the gift. The tax is not on the property itself; it is on the right to make a gift. The tax rates for transfers by gift and transfers through an estate are exactly the same. With the unified transfer approach to taxes we now have, there is no advantage from a tax rate standpoint to making gifts while a person is alive versus passing property on death. As we will see later, however, there are some very significant economic advantages to transferring property by gift rather than waiting to do it on death.

Let's now look at how gifts are actually taxed. Remember, with the unified transfer approach to taxes, the tax rate for gift taxes and estate taxes is the same.

The gift tax is computed by determining the total lifetime transfers in excess of the annual exclusion per year per beneficiary. That tax rate is then applied to the tax tables which yields a tentative tax. From that tentative tax is deducted the amount of any prior gift taxes paid by the individual. Also deducted is the unified credit for the year of the gift in tax credits. The tax tables are found in Appendix H. Before turning to these, it is important to see how they work. This complicated-sounding formula can be broken down into meaningful concepts so taxes can be readily computed. The formula will serve to determine not only the gift taxes but also the estate taxes. For the Floridian concerned about paying gift or estate taxes, it is essential to master this formula, however intimidating it may seem at first. Let's walk through the formula, starting with some of the simpler concepts.

Annual Exclusion

Every person can give away up to $10,000 per year per beneficiary free of tax. This $10,000 is called the annual exclusion and is indexed for inflation with the year 1997 as the base or starting year. This means that gifts under the inflation-adjusted $10,000 per year per beneficiary fall into the birthday gift category and are not going to cause a gift tax to arise or even require that a gift tax return be filed. If it's under the adjusted $10,000 and an outright gift, the government considers this too small to be reported. Therefore, any of these annual exclusion gifts per recipient do not enter into the formula above.

Two Considerations on Annual Exclusion Gifts

When contemplating making an annual exclusion gift, it is important to remember that the gift must be of a "present interest." Gifts that are not of a present interest do not qualify for the annual exclusion and must be reported on a gift tax return. Present interest means that the beneficiary must have the present right to the gift. A gift of $10,000 in which the beneficiary gets the income or principal five years from now is not a gift of a present interest. It is a gift of the money in the future—a future interest. There is another very important consideration. No one, through eagerness to be generous or to avoid estate taxes, should so deplete his or her own estate as to become dependent on someone else. The child should never become the parent. The parent should never become the child. The pleasures of giving and of seeing the benefits derived from your gifts are wonderful, but financial dependency arising out of unanticipated expense or financial reverses must always be considered.

Annual exclusion gifts each year to a number of people can significantly reduce estate taxes and cause no gift tax to arise. Let's look at another big tax savings item.

The Equivalent Exemption or Exempt Amount

Congress has determined that every US citizen should have the right to transfer some property free of any gift or estate tax. This is known as the equivalent exemption. It is the amount that can pass free of tax—estate or gift. This exempt amount is adjusted each year. Unlike the $10,000 annual exclusion which is only adjusted for inflation, the exempt amount is automatically increased each year as follows:

1998	$625,000
1999	$650,000
2000	$675,000
2001	$675,000
2002	$700,000
2003	$700,000
2004	$850,000
2005	$950,000
2006	$1,000,000

Unlike the annual exclusion, however, which renews itself every year, the equivalent exemption is one that may be used either in whole or in part in any way, but does not in any way renew itself.

It is easy to think in terms of the equivalent exemption as a deduction because most taxpayers are used to thinking in terms of deductions before the tax is calculated. Actually, in the case of the $600,000+ deduction, this is something of a misnomer. Technically speaking, there really is no $600,000 deduction, although the law works as though there were. What really happens is that each US citizen has a tax credit against gift or estate taxes of $192,800. Under the tax tables, it turns out that if a person gives away $600,000, the tax on this gift is $192,800. Since that person has a tax credit of $192,800 which goes against the tax due of $192,800, there is no actual tax to be paid, but the tax credit has now exactly been eaten up by the tax. This $600,000+ is called the equivalent exemption because it is the equivalent amount that is exempt from taxes because of the tax credit. For most of our purposes when we are thinking about estate planning for Floridians, we will think and talk about a deduction rather than a tax credit. It is easier to think about the $600,000+ as being a deduction which every US citizen is born with and can spend during his or her lifetime in giving gifts or on death in passing property so that this $600,000+ worth of transferred property is not subject to any gift or estate tax.

Let's see how this might work out when we apply a simple set of facts to these complex tax laws. In 1997, Jim made gifts to his two daughters, Linda and Carol. He wanted to treat both children equally, but he knew that Linda wanted to go into business and needed some extra capital to get her new business started. Therefore, he decided that he would give each of them $50,000 for a total of $100,000. He realized that he was over his annual exclusion amount of $10,000 so there would be some tax implications.

Jim had not made any previous taxable gifts, so he started with his full $600,000 (1997) exemption. Because of the annual exclusion, he deducted his 1997 annual exclusion of $10,00 per year per beneficiary. This meant he deducted the $10,000 annual exclusion gift to Linda and the $10,000 annual exclusion gift to Carol. He made, for tax purposes, a reportable gift of $50,000 less the $10,000 annual exclusion gift—or $40,000—to Linda and a similar $40,000 gift to Carol. He had a $600,000 exemption to be used either in whole or in part during his lifetime so he applied the $80,000 reportable gifts ($40,000 times 2) against his $600,000 exemption. Thus he paid no gift tax on his gift of $100,000 to the girls. However, he used up all of his annual exclusion for that year of $10,000 each, and the $80,000 was deducted from his 1997 $600,000 lifetime exemption, leaving him with a remaining balance of $520,000. If he made no other taxable gifts during his lifetime, then on Jim's death, his estate will be taxable after using the equivalent exemption for the year of his death and deducting the excess of his annual gifts to the two girls. The excess was $80,000, so $80,000 is the amount that is deducted from the amount that can pass tax free on his death. He has used up part of his equivalent exemption amount by making the extra large annual gift.

Remember that there is an annual exclusion of $10,000 adjusted for inflation per giver per beneficiary, that gifts to a spouse are tax-free, and that anybody can also transfer up to the equivalent exemption free of estate tax or gift tax, and you'll have a good working grasp of how the gift and estate tax law works.

Deductions

Other deductions are available besides the equivalent exemption and the annual exclusion. We'll cover these in more detail, but essentially these are gifts to charities, certain gifts to pay the medical expenses or tuition of another person, and the largest of all deductions—gifts to a spouse who is a US citizen.

The Marital Deduction

The federal government treats a husband and wife for gift tax purposes generally as a single economic unit. This means that, for gift purposes, property may be freely transferred between a husband and wife with no gift tax implications. You may transfer as much as you wish to your spouse. There's no tax and, in fact, no gift tax return is required. You simply can transfer assets between the two of you as you both consider best. The significance of this is great. In estate planning, the ability to shift assets between a husband and a wife without any gift tax arising provides us with many opportunities for changing the management of the assets and for saving estate taxes. We will look at some of these opportunities on a case-by-case basis later on, but for now, it is important to remember that assets can be freely transferred between a husband and a wife without any gift tax.

The Charitable Deduction

Most everyone knows that if you make a gift to charity, you can take a deduction for this gift. The deduction shows up on your income tax return for the value of the gift that you made to the charity. When it comes to estate planning, however, there's another important rule: You can make a gift to a charity and have it escape taxation on your death, and you can still retain certain rights in the gifted assets while you are alive. This becomes very important when we want the charity to get the benefit of our gift in the future, but in the meantime, we want to retain the use of the property or retain the right to receive the income. We'll explore this ability to give an asset to a charity with a retained right and how that works under the gift tax, estate tax, and income tax laws with the complex types of trusts known as Grantor Retained Annuity Trust and Grantor Retained Unitrust (see Chapter 14).

Medical and Tuition Exclusion

The Internal Revenue Code includes an exclusion that might be called a loophole, yet it is a very desirable provision for many. If a gift is made for medical care or tuition and is done correctly, there is no gift tax at all. There is no annual exclusion calculation, and there is no equivalent exemption calculation. A person may make unlimited gifts to benefit another person for tuition or for medical care.

Tuition means tuition costs in the more traditional and restricted sense of fees for education. It does not include food, lodging, books, and similar items. Medical care means medical care in the usual sense and in fact is technically defined in the Internal Revenue Code. To qualify for the provision that says there is no gift tax for payments for tuition or medical care, the payments must be made directly to the provider of the services. It will not work if you give a check to the child for tuition purposes: The checks must be made out directly to the college or university or to the health care provider.

Gifts with a Spouse or Split Gifts

There is a benefit to having a spouse when it comes to making gifts. Earlier, we said the Federal government treated a husband and wife as a single economic unit for many purposes. This means your spouse can join you in making gifts and thereby reduce the tax effect by half. For example, if you wanted to make a gift of $20,000 to your sister, you would have to file a gift tax return on the amount over the annual exclusion amount. However, the gift tax law permits your spouse to join in the gift ("gift splitting") and treats your $20,000 gift as being made by both of you. This $20,000 from you (and your spouse) is like $10,000 each. Since each person has the annual exclusion, this means no tax at all. If just one person had made the $20,000 gift, that means $20,000 minus the annual exclusion would be taxed. It is necessary, however, to file a gift tax return to indicate a "split gift." This is a very short gift tax return and is very simple to prepare.

Making Gifts Today

It is often better from an estate tax planning standpoint to make a gift while you're alive. While the value of the gift is charged against the total amount that can be given tax free, all future appreciation on the gift—including dividends, interest income, capital gains and other increases in value—will occur outside the giver's estate. These increases now belong to the recipient. Therefore, the value of the gift given while you're alive is usually worth much more than the same amount inherited after your death.

A Gift Is a Gift, with No Strings Attached

In order for a gift to really be a gift, it is important to make it with no strings attached. It is extremely easy for the Internal Revenue Service to find a way to argue that the giver of the gift kept a string or condition of some type on a gift. The Internal Revenue Service will say that it is not a completed gift if the giver still had the right to control the beneficial enjoyment of this gift in any way, to any degree. Since it is not a completed gift, it is still included in the giver's estate and subject to estate tax. When this happens, things become even more difficult. The person who received the gift doesn't have to give it back. But the estate still has to pay the tax because the gifted property is included in the estate because of the string. The people paying the estate tax may not be the same ones who received the gift. The estate beneficiaries paying this extra estate tax will feel that they are being forced to pay the taxes on something they did not get.

Ray and Lisa were married late in life. Lisa promised Ray that if he would will a substantial part of his assets to her, she would make sure that his kids got his money when she died. Ray died and left a very large estate to Lisa. Ray's children talked Lisa into setting up an irrevocable trust with the property which she inherited from Ray. Under the terms of the trust, she kept the income for her lifetime. On her death, the assets were to go to Ray's children under the terms of the trust.

Lisa died and problems began to surface. The terms of the trust provided for the assets in the trust to go to Ray's children, and so they did. On the other hand, Lisa had kept a string. She had kept the income for life. Therefore, the assets in the trust were included in her estate for tax purposes. A substantial estate tax had to be paid from Lisa's estate. The estate taxes came out of her assets passing under her will. In fact, the taxes were so high they ate up Lisa's own small estate. Ray's children came out pretty well: They got all of Ray's property tax free. Lisa's children got nothing. The taxes took everything she personally owned.

Filing the Gift Tax Return

If a gift tax return is due, almost all individual taxpayers must file the gift tax return on April 15. It should be filed in the same place where the federal income tax return is filed. In computing the tax, all prior taxable gifts are taken into account so that the gift tax is cumulative and the equivalent exemption will continue to be reduced.

Summary

Gifts can be made of $10,000 per year per giver per beneficiary, and there is no tax as long as the gift is a gift of a present interest. This $10,000 is adjusted annually for inflation by rounding down to the nearest $1,000. Making a gift keeps the property out of the giver's estate as long as the giver doesn't attach any strings to the gift. Gifts of annual exclusion amounts can be very beneficial in reducing the size of the estate and seeing how well beneficiaries manage the property they are given. It is important to always keep some money aside for unforeseen expenses such as medical care, changes in personal finances, or a poor economy.

What's necessary is to determine the amount of the gift and then deduct the annual exclusion amount of $10,000 per recipient (or $20,000 per recipient if a spouse is included in the gift-giving). The balance is the equivalent exemption amount that is unused. In most instances, this is reduced as gifts in excess of the annual exclusion amounts are given. Gifts to a spouse who is a US citizen are always free of tax and can be very useful in estate planning.

When making a major gift, it is important to be aware that the gift should be a complete gift without any strings attached unless it is a special kind of gift to a charity. Otherwise, unforeseen tax results could occur which can cause problems. All in all, the gift tax law is more simple than it appears to be at first. With proper use, it can produce not only excellent gift tax results, but also excellent estate tax results. It can also provide the donor with great pleasure in seeing beneficiaries enjoy the gifts and with satisfaction in helping others.

In this chapter, you will learn about:

- federal estate tax in general
- the taxation of specific types of assets
- alternate valuation
- deductions
- funeral expenses and expenses in administering the estate
- debts of decedent, mortgages, and loans
- bequests to a surviving spouse
- charitable gifts
- tax credits
- credit for prior transfers
- unified transfers
- the Florida estate tax pattern
- how to figure Florida's estate tax
- gift tax and estate tax transfer tax

9

ESTATE TAXES IN A NUTSHELL

Federal Estate Tax

The estate tax works in a way similar to the gift tax. Like the gift tax, the estate tax is levied on the right or privilege of transferring property after death. It is not a tax on the property itself.

For tax purposes, the estate is composed of everything a person owns. Uncle Sam throws a very broad net, and that net has very, very small holes. Almost nothing escapes his definition of the taxable estate. Not only does it include property and property interests which the decedent (person who died) owned at the time of death, it also includes property transferred by the decedent but in which he or she retained any type of interest or string, however small, by way of receiving income or keeping power to change the enjoyment of the property (remember Lisa from the previous chapter).

Incidentally, "tax-free assets" means tax-free for income tax purposes.

There's no such thing as tax-free when it comes to estate taxes. It is all taxable. Don't be misled into believing that the phrase "tax-free" means it is free from estate tax as well.

Real Estate

In computing the estate tax, Uncle Sam insists that everything that a decedent owned or had an ownership interest in be listed on the estate tax return. Assets such as real estate must be listed, and, in almost all instances, appraisals must be done and must show the fair market value.

Stocks and Bonds

All stocks and bonds of any type, including tax-free bonds, must be shown on the estate tax return at their fair market value. In instances such as closely held corporations, the corporation stock is valued using appropriate formulas. In the case of widely traded securities such as IBM and General Motors, the values that are used will be the average of the high and the low of the stock during the day in which the decedent passed away. If the decedent passed away on a holiday or weekend, then the average of the high and low values on the trading day before and the trading day after are used for valuation purposes. Some bonds, such as municipal bonds, can be a bit difficult to value and require some specialized services. Municipal bonds are not usually printed in the newspaper daily as are nationally traded stocks.

Mortgages, Notes, and Cash

All mortgages, notes, and cash must be listed for tax purposes. Any promissory notes due the decedent must be valued at the fair market value. In instances where the interest rate on the note is high, the note may have a value higher than the outstanding principal balance. Conversely, if the interest rate is very low, then the promissory note may have a value less than the outstanding principal balance. Promissory notes and mortgages may also be discounted if there is a real possibility that the debtor may not pay off the note.

Insurance

Insurance is subject to estate tax, and, in fact, it is one of the most easily taxed items by the federal government for estate tax purposes. Any insurance owned by the decedent must be listed. This means that insurance which the decedent owned on someone else's life must also be included on the decedent's estate tax return. Conversely, insurance on the decedent's life but owned by someone other than the decedent is reported for informational purposes but is not actually taxed in the decedent's estate.

Jointly Owned Property

Jointly owned property is included in the decedent's estate for estate tax purposes. While joint property may not pass through probate, it is certainly taxed. If the property was owned jointly between the decedent and the spouse, then only one-half of the value of the jointly held property is included for tax purposes because of the marital share rules. If there is jointly held property with persons other than a spouse, then all the jointly held property must be included in the decedent's estate. The full value of the property held jointly by a person other than a spouse must be included in the decedent's estate unless it can be proved that the surviving cotenant contributed to the jointly owned property. If there was contribution by the surviving cotenant, then the amount included in the decedent's estate is not 100%, but just the proportion the decedent contributed. Joint property means (1) any joint interest which the decedent had either in real estate, personal property (both tangible and intangible), or bank accounts; or (2) any other type of jointly held property in which the decedent had an ownership interest either as joint tenant with right of survivorship or as a tenant by the entirety.

Miscellaneous Interests Included in the Estate

Since there can be other items which would be included in the decedent's estate, the IRS tax return includes a blanket request that anything owned by the decedent that is not reported elsewhere must be included on the estate tax return. This would typically include items such as tangible personal property or any other interests that the decedent might have had.

Items of tangible personal property, such as artistic items, with a value of $3,000 must also be specifically listed. Any collections which have a combined value of $10,000 must be specifically listed with appropriate appraisals as well.

Transfers During Decedent's Life

Complete transfers made by a decedent during lifetime generally are not included. However, if the decedent made any kind of transfer and retained any type of interest or string, then the decedent's estate must include this transfer. A common example of this is a person who gives away tax-free municipal bonds but keeps the coupons. This is an incomplete transfer in terms of the estate tax law. It is treated as a transfer with a retained income interest. The entire value of those tax-free municipal bonds at the time of death would be included in the giver's estate. Earlier we saw in the case of Lisa that she had transferred her late husband's property to an irrevocable trust, but she retained the right to receive the income during her lifetime; thus the full value of those assets was included in her estate, even though she had an income interest only.

Other types of transfers—such as when a person makes a gift but retains the right to direct how the gift will be used, or makes a gift to a group of people but retains the right to direct which members of that group shall enjoy the gift—are also counted at full value. Any of these retained rights would cause the gifts to be incomplete for tax purposes, and such a transfer during a decedent's life would cause the entire value of the property to be brought back into the estate. It's not just the retained right that is taxed; it's the entire value of the property. Certainly, assets put into a typical living trust would be included in the decedent's estate tax return and typically would be included under the section reporting transfers during the decedent's life with a retained income interest.

The Three-Year Rule and Gifts in Contemplation of Death

It is very difficult to find an asset not subject to tax. Insurance policies are included. In fact, even life insurance policies that the decedent gave away within three years of death are still included in this tax. However, the old rule which said that any other gifts made within three years were deemed to be "in contemplation of death" has gone. With the unified gift and estate tax tables, the old 25% advantage of making gifts is gone. Under the old rule, *any* gift made within three years of the death of the giver was generally included in the giver's estate.

Powers of Appointment

Sometimes, for estate planning purposes, by will one spouse will give the other spouse the right to direct where the first spouse's property will go upon the death of the second spouse. A couple might decide that the surviving spouse should decide which of the children would receive the assets and in what amounts. This is known as a limited or special power of appointment and is not taxed in the second spouse's estate for estate tax purposes. However, it *is* property taxed in the first spouse's estate. If the power is much broader than this and the surviving spouse can also use the assets to pay his or her bills or could will the power of appointment property to anyone, then this is considered to be a general power of appointment and, as such, all the value of the property would be included in the second spouse's estate for tax purposes.

Annuities

Annuities are included for estate tax purposes. The value of the annuity that's included is the fair market value of the right to receive the distributions that remain after the decedent's death. For example, a brother might purchase an annuity with all the income coming to him during his lifetime; upon his death, his sister is to receive the balance of his annuity payments. If the brother dies, his estate must include the value of this annuity on his death since he was receiving the income and there was a remaining value on the annuity which was equal to the payments the surviving sister will receive over her lifetime (adjusted to reflect that the payments are spread out over some time in the future and therefore should be reduced to equal a current value).

Alternate Valuation

The estate tax law has an unusual provision in it. There are two or three valuation dates that can be used in determining the total value. The date of death is first used as a valuation date. Six months later, the entire estate may be revalued and, if there is tax due, the revaluation figures may be selected. A third valuation date—when an asset is sold—may also be used. It is not uncommon in estates for stocks and bonds to be sold during the course of administration. If these stocks and bonds are sold within the first six months after death, then the valuation date for these securities may be the value on the day that they were actually sold. Unfortunately, the Internal Revenue Service will not let you choose whether some assets can take the date-of-death value and others can take the date six months later. The return must be consistent and show the same valuation date throughout, except in the instance where assets were sold. Then the valuation date as of the date of sale may be used if the alternate valuation's date is used for the other assets.

Deductions

We've seen that Uncle Sam includes for taxes everything that a person might own at the time of death, even partial interests. In some instances, just retained rights such as income rights could cause the entire value of the income and the principal to be included in the decedent's estate. What are some of the deductions that can be used for estate tax purposes?

Funeral Expenses and Expenses Incurred in Administering the Estate

Funeral expenses are certainly deductible, as are executors' fees, attorneys' fees, accountants' fees, and miscellaneous expenses incurred in maintaining the property during the time that the estate is being administered prior to distribution to the beneficiaries.

Debts of the Decedent, Mortgages, and Loans

The decedent's debts—for example, funeral bills and mortgages on property—can be deducted on the estate tax return.

Bequests to a Surviving Spouse

Just as in the gift tax area, assets passing to a spouse are free of estate tax. Any asset that passed to a surviving spouse outright is deducted from the estate tax return, provided the surviving spouse is a US citizen. If the asset does not pass outright to the surviving spouse, then the property may or may not be deductible depending upon certain technical qualifications. We'll discuss these qualifications concerning Qualified Terminable Interest Property (QTIP) and similar advanced concepts in Chapter 12, but for now anything that passes to a surviving spouse is free of estate tax and may be deducted on the estate tax return.

Charitable Gifts

As on your income tax return and gift tax return, charitable gifts are deductible. Unlike the income tax rules, there's no limitation on the deductions for charitable gifts on an estate tax return. Anything that passes to a charity may be deducted at its full market value at the time of death.

Tax Credits

Tax credits are more valuable than deductions—at least on a dollar-for-dollar basis—because the deduction simply reduces the value of the estate, whereas a tax credit is like actual money you can spend. A deduction of $100,000 might be worth $55,000 in real money in an estate that was in the 55% bracket, but a tax credit of $100,000 is worth $100,000. Two types of tax credits are sometimes seen when looking at the estate. One is a credit for foreign death tax. Taxes paid to a foreign country may be deductible in accordance with treaties between the US and that foreign country.

Credit for Prior Transfers

The other tax credit is for property which has been subjected to US estate tax within ten years. The government does not think it's fair that it gets two full bites of the (estate) apple within ten years. Accordingly, if property has been taxed within ten years, then a tax credit for the estate tax previously paid is allowed on the subsequent estate tax return. This tax credit decreases as the interval between the two estate tax returns approaches ten years. For property that was subjected to estate taxes within the first two years, then the estate tax credit allowed on the subsequent return for taxes paid on the prior return is 100%. This drops to 80% for property that was taxed between two and four years later, to 60% for property that was taxed between four and six years later, to 40% for property that was taxed six and eight years later, and finally to 20% for property that was taxed eight to ten years later. If the property was taxed ten or more years ago, then no credit is allowed.

Unified Transfers

As we saw in the prior chapter concerning gift taxes, there's a unified rate concerning estate and gift taxes. The tax, known as a transfer tax, is exactly the same if you pass property by will or if you transfer it as a gift. The tax is computed after adding up all the property the decedent had, together with any interest that would be taxable in the decedent's estate. From this are taken the deductions indicated in this chapter. If the decedent has made any gifts in excess of the annual exclusion gifts of $10,000 as adjusted per year per beneficiary, then this will have been reducing the decedent's equivalent exemption increased by the tables for the year of death. If there have been no gifts in excess of $10,000 as adjusted per year per beneficiary, then the decedent would of course have the full equivalent exemption for the appropriate year of the decedent's death still available.

The Florida Estate Tax Pattern

The Florida estate tax pattern is almost identical to the federal estate tax pattern. Florida does not even have an estate tax return—it uses a copy of the federal estate tax return. This return is due at the same time as the federal one, nine months from the date of death. The payment for each is due when the return is filed. The state return is filed with the Florida Department of Revenue in Tallahassee. Florida relies almost exclusively on the Internal Revenue Service's auditing procedures, practices, and personnel. If the federal estate tax return is accepted by the Internal Revenue Service, it will, in almost all instances, be accepted by the state of Florida. Conversely, if the Internal Revenue Service challenges the estate tax return on audit and successfully determines that more tax is due, Florida will increase its tax proportionately.

Florida's Estate Tax

Florida's tax is based on a provision of the federal law which says that, within certain limitations, amounts paid to a state can be credited against federal estate tax. If, for instance, federal law says that the federal estate tax on a million-dollar estate is $153,000, the federal government would give a credit of approximately $38,000 on this liability for taxes paid to a state. Florida takes advantage of this and says that the Florida tax on such an estate of approximately one million dollars will be equal to the federal credit, or around $38,000. The net result is that the estate owes $153,000 by reason of the decedent's death. The federal estate tax is $153,000. However, if $38,000 of this is paid to the state of Florida, then only $115,000 need be paid directly to the federal government. It is an unusual kind of tax that doesn't cost you anything extra.

Many times, people will say, "Florida has no estate tax." Technically, it does have an estate tax. However, since the Florida estate tax is included in the federal tax, you do not have to pay any extra tax. So, since you don't pay any extra, it is as though there is no tax. Almost all other states have some type of estate tax—usually higher. Some states follow Florida's example of having their tax equal to the federal credit. Only one state, Nevada, has no estate tax whatsoever.

Gift Tax and Estate Tax=Transfer Tax

We have talked about gift taxes and estate taxes, both to the federal government and to the state of Florida. The important thing to remember about the transfer tax is that it's unified. The tax rates are the same whether you give property during your life or after your death. The taxes are going to be the same. The first $600,000+, adjusted for the increase for the year of death, is tax-free. Annual gifts of $10,000, adjusted for inflation per person, do not count against this $600,000. The estate and gift tax rates are the highest rates you are likely to encounter.

Summary

The Florida and federal estate tax return is due nine months from the date of death unless an extension is granted. The estate tax return is very lengthy and should be completed only by an experienced person. The estate tax return for a taxable estate will show a great deal of tax liability because the tax rates are high and because these high rates are applied to everything, not just income. It is important to employ someone who is thoroughly familiar with these complex returns; there is too much money involved to skimp. Ask your tax preparer how many estate tax returns (Form 706) he or she has prepared in the last three years. This will give you an idea of how familiar he or she is with these complex tax returns.

In this chapter, you will learn about:

- gifts in excess of $600,000
- magic of compounding
- what to give
- property with high growth potential
- business interests
- high basis property
- the step up in basis
- joint property and the step up in basis
- gifts of life insurance
- gifts in contemplation of death
- disclaimers, or "thanks but no thanks"
- the common disaster

10

BEYOND THE BASICS

We've looked at both gift taxes and estate taxes in a nutshell. Now it's time to put some of these concepts into use. How can we apply the gift tax and estate tax in such a way as to get the best tax result and the best "people" result? We'll start off with some of the gift tax approaches to learn how to make tax-smart gifts.

Gifts in Excess of the Exempt Amount

In the chapter on gifts, we talked about annual exclusion gifts of $10,000 adjusted for inflation per year per beneficiary. We noted that gifts in excess of a total of $600,000+ (the equivalent exemption adjusted for the year of the gift or death, other than the annual exclusion gifts) were subject to gift tax. Is it a good idea for a person who has substantial assets to consider making gifts in excess of $600,000+ even though this causes some tax to actually be paid? The answer is yes.

Financially successful and generous people frequently make gifts that exceed $600,000+. Now the tax begins to be real. The total amount of gifts made in all preceding years is added up and the total amount of taxes due on the total gifts is calculated. Any prior gift taxes paid and the unified credit for the applicable year are deducted from the total tax due. The result is the tax due for that particular year.

For example, let's suppose that Paul had made a gift of $500,000 in 1995. He would not have paid a gift tax because he would have been using up his tax-free $600,000. Paul had a good year in 1997 and makes a gift of an additional $250,000. Now his total gifts are $750,000. The tax in 1997 on $750,000 was $248,300. He still has the unified tax credit of $192,800. This is subtracted from the $248,300, so the tax he has to send the federal government is $55,500. A check is made payable to the Internal Revenue Service and the tax return is filed on or before April 15. If Paul has another good year, and after making annual exclusion gifts, he makes another $250,000 gift, he would have made total gifts of $1,000,000. The total tax would be $345,800, but from that would be subtracted the $192,800 tax credit and the $55,500 previously paid. The tax due on the additional $250,000 would be $97,500. If Paul had made his additional gift in 1998 instead of 1997, his $600,000 equivalent exemption would have increased in 1998 by $25,000 (see page 211) and would have become $625,000 with a resulting reduction in the tax. Then again, maybe the assets, if gifted in 1997, would have appreciated more than the entire tax in 1997 and the beneficiary would be better off.

Magic of Compounding

One estate planning idea that works well is that the value of a gift today is worth far more than a gift of the same dollar amount in the future. A gift today has the opportunity to grow and grow, free of any estate tax. Property kept will also grow and grow, but then on death can be subject to tax on the final large amount. The amount can be surprising. A dollar given *each year*, assuming a net annual growth rate of 5% over 15 years, will produce a total of more than $21. That's a staggering increase when you think about it.

A $10,000 gift given *each year* for 15 years will compound and grow to $210,000 in 15 years if an annual sustained yield of 5% after taxes can be obtained. Twenty years of gifts makes the gifts 33 times more valuable.

If the gift were not made, the retained money and growth occur in the giver's estate. Since the gift is never made, the money will be subject to estate taxes. The estate taxes may be 55%. Because of this phenomenon, people frequently make annual exclusion gifts, and wealthy individuals make gifts of more than the equivalent exemption. This is true even though the gift may cause a tax to be paid. Thereafter, the gifted property can grow and not be subject to estate taxes, so that the equivalent exemption becomes "leveraged." In 15 years, a one-time gift of $600,000 at 5% net growth is worth more than $1,200,000; a 10% growth rate makes $600,000 grow to more than $2,500,000!

What to Give

If gift giving is such a great idea, what types of property should you give? Deciding what to give frequently can be as challenging as deciding how much to give. One of the easiest things to give is cash, but it is also one of the most expensive. After all, you probably had to pay income tax on the cash. This may have meant selling something and paying capital gains tax on it. Frequently, a gift of something other than cash, such as income-producing property, is better. More often than not, the person who makes the gift is in a higher income tax bracket than the person who receives it. If this is the case, isn't it better to have the income earned in the future paid by the person in the lower bracket rather than the person in the higher bracket?

Property with High Growth Potential

This is a great choice for making gifts. After all, you get it out of the estate at a low rate because it hasn't reached its maximum growth yet. Not only does it come out of the estate at a lower rate, but also the growth occurs outside the taxable estate of the giver. At the time of the death of the giver, it may be worth many, many times the original investment. Yet there is no tax on it.

Sometimes, however, property goes the other way. Property that is shrinking in value, or property that is technically known as a wasting asset, is not a good choice for a gift. The property, if gifted, would come out at a high cost and have a relatively low value at the time of death, offering little tax savings. Some assets naturally shrink: gifts of copyright interests, patents, and interests such as mineral rights. These should not be given as gifts. Keep them and let them be taxed at the low value in an estate.

Closely Held Business Interests

Closely held business interests make interesting gifts. They are interesting because (a) they frequently have a considerable value, (b) they have a considerable potential for appreciation, and (c) they can do some unusually positive things in the donor's estate. Let's look at what happens to the owner of a closely held business who decides he would like to make gifts to a number of beneficiaries. Ric has been the sole owner of a very successful car dealership for many years. He really would like to start phasing out of this hectic business and to have the children take over. He decides that he is going to make gifts each year to the children of portions of his interest in the business. Ric is married and will be doing some gift-splitting, or having his wife, Gina, join in the gifts. This means that Ric and Gina will be able to distribute $20,000 worth of interest in the business each year to each of their five children. They will be able to distribute $100,000 a year tax-free to the children. Ric does this over a number of years, and gradually his ownership in the car business shrinks. As it does, there will come a time when he will have given away a little more than half the value of the total outstanding stock in the business. Ric is no longer a majority shareholder. This is an emotional time and must be very carefully considered by him, by the children, and by Ric's estate planners.

Once Ric has made the leap and is a minority interest shareholder, he probably will have some sense of loss, but to make up for this, a very beneficial effect has taken place for tax purposes. When Ric dies, the estate tax value of his minority interest will be substantially discounted from its numerical value. For example, let's suppose that at the time of Ric's death, he owns 30% of the stock and that the business has a net fair market value of $2,000,000. This means that the numerical value of his stock would be $600,000. But because Ric had a minority interest in a closely held, family type of corporation, a very strong argument can be made that his estate should be entitled to a discount because he was a minority shareholder. It is entirely likely that this discount would be at least 25%. Therefore, the 25% discount applied to his interest of $600,000 means that, for tax purposes, his stock is valued at only $450,000. In addition, other discounts may be argued for on the grounds that the asset is illiquid and should be discounted because of the lack of marketability. Thus Ric has been able to shift ownership of the business, as well as a tremendous amount of taxability away from his estate, over to his children, and he never had to pay any gift tax on the gifted assets. He also was able to push down the remaining value of his stock so that there was little or no tax on that as well.

High Basis Property

Basis of property means the value which the Internal Revenue Service determined to be the basis or value of the property in computing your federal income taxes. For income tax purposes, we are more familiar with how basis works. If a person buys stock for $10 a share and sells it for $15 a share, there is a capital gain of $5 a share. This capital gain is computed on the basis. The basis is the value paid for the stock. Basis may be either higher or lower than fair market value. If the stock had been purchased for $15 a share and was sold for $10 a share, the basis would still be $15 a share, and a capital loss of $5 would have been recognized. For gift tax purposes, the government's rule is "heads I win, tails you lose."

If a person makes a gift of an asset, the basis in the hands of a recipient is the same basis that the donor owned: if stock was purchased for $10 a share, and at the time it was given was worth $15, the recipient of the property takes the gift with the old basis of $10, but the government *taxes* the gift to the donor at its fair market value at the time of the gift—$15. Therefore, the government collects more gift tax because of the higher value placed on the gift. It also has the capital gain tax still to be collected at some future date when the recipient sells the stock and has to pay capital gains based on the old basis (the donor's basis) of $10. For federal estate tax purposes, it is a little more even-handed.

For federal estate tax purposes, property is valued at its fair market value as of the time of death or in some instances on an alternate valuation date. The basis of inherited property is its fair market value as of the date of death or alternate valuation date. This means that all prior capital appreciation that had occurred in an asset up until the time of a person's death will not be taxed. If, in the example above, a person had bought stock at $10 a share and at the time of death the stock was worth $15 a share, it is taxed for estate tax purposes as having a value of $15. In this case, unlike the gift tax, the beneficiary receives the stock at its fair market value as of the date of death, or $15 a share, and receives what is known as a step up in basis.

If the gift is of highly appreciated property, it may be better not to make the gift. The reason lies in the provisions concerning capital gains. If a person dies with an asset, it doesn't matter what was paid for that asset. The estate receives a *stepped up basis*. Anyone who inherits that property could sell the property shortly after receiving it and recognize no capital gains. The person who died would have recognized capital gains had he or she sold the property between the date of purchase and the date of death, but the only capital gain the beneficiary has to pay is on the gain *after* death. George had a cost basis in Coca Cola stock of $10 per share. Coca Cola was selling for $60 at the time of his death. If George had sold his stock, he would have recognized $50 worth of capital gain on the Coca Cola sale. On the other hand, since George died owning the Coca Cola stock, when his beneficiaries receive the stock, the beneficiaries receive it at a tax basis of $60, the value as of the date of death. This means that George's beneficiaries of the Coca Cola stock could sell the stock the next day and recognize no capital gains whatsoever. This rule applies to all assets that are inherited, whether by will or by trust.

Conversely, however, if a person is unfortunate enough to have some property that has gone down in value, the same rule applies—that is, all capital loss disappears as well. This leads us to an estate planning insight that may be expressed as a rule: If a person has a terminal illness, it is better to sell an asset in which he or she has a loss and hold on to any assets that have gains. The losses can be recognized for income tax purposes and the gains will disappear and never be taxed on death.

There are some exceptions to this step up in basis. One of the exceptions is on jointly held property. Property jointly held with a spouse may be considered to be only 50% owned by the deceased so there is only a 50% step up in basis. For property gifted *to* the deceased within one year before his or her death and then inherited back by the giver, there is no step up in basis at all. When considering the lifetime strategies for making gifts, it is a good idea to give income-producing property to beneficiaries who are in low income brackets. It is a good idea to avoid selling assets and recognizing capital gain in order to make gifts. It is especially important not to make gifts if the giver has an extremely low basis in these assets and it is likely that the giver will die in the reasonably near future. Making a gift of this type of asset is making a gift to the Internal Revenue Service.

Gifts of Life Insurance

A gift of life insurance also has a peculiar rule. The Internal Revenue Service loves to tax life insurance, so much so that special rules have been passed by Congress making it easier to tax life insurance. After all, life insurance is inherently associated with death. There normally is a large amount of money involved, and it is cash. These factors combine to make the insurance policy proceeds look especially appealing to the tax collector. One of the special rules passed provides that, if a person owns a life insurance policy and makes a gift of that policy within *three* years before death, the full value of that policy is going to be included in the estate, even though the deceased person does not actually own the insurance anymore. This is an echo of the old three-year "contemplation of death" rule, but now the calendar settles all arguments. Did the person own the life insurance policy? Did he or she make a gift of the policy? Did he or she die within three years? If the answer to these three questions is yes, then the answer to the fourth question—"Is that policy subject to estate tax?"—is always going to be yes.

Using Gifts to Change the Tax Basis

Sometimes a close family member is in very poor health. If that family member has a relatively modest estate and if it appears that, although he or she is in poor health, he or she will live at least a year longer, it may be wise to make a gift to that person. This may sound a bit macabre, yet we have to deal with the reality of taxes and death. Under the income tax law, an inheritance has a new income tax basis unless the inherited property was given *to* the decedent within one year of the decedent's death. A gift of property with a very low basis given to a person with a relatively modest estate can produce a significant tax savings. The person receives the gift and lives more than one year. At the time of death, the property receives a step up in basis. All prior capital gain has disappeared. The gifted property can be willed back to the giver with a brand new tax basis and no capital gains tax to pay.

Alternatively, if it appears that the recipient may not live a year, it is still possible to make a tax-wise gift. It is just not permissible to will the property back to the giver. As long as it does not come back to the giver of the property, the step up in basis still applies. The property could then be willed to the children or other persons to be benefited. How many people's circumstances may fit this situation and how many people choose to use this device will be a matter of circumstance, timing, and, yes, sensitivity. It is included here because it is something that many people want to consider.

Disclaimers, or a Way of Saying "Thanks but No Thanks"

The disclaimer is one of the tools used occasionally in estate planning. It is a way of saying "Thank you, but no thank you," or "I do not wish to receive this inheritance." Disclaimers are frequently used for tax purposes or for other valid considerations. They are recognized under both federal law and Florida law. When properly used, they can provide significant tax savings. The disclaimer must be made within nine months from the date of death. Some formalities must be closely adhered to if the disclaimer is going to work for federal estate tax purposes. Let's look at an example in which a disclaimer might be appropriate.

A Typical Disclaimer Situation

Suppose we have a couple, Monte and Anne. When Anne dies, the total assets in her estate are worth $600,000 and are all willed to Monte. Monte has no particular need for this kind of money. He has an estate of $800,000 himself. Because of his inheriting Anne's property, Monte's total estate will be $1,400,000 or more. The tax on his death could be $320,000. That's a whopping amount of tax that the children will have to pay within nine months of Monte's death.

Is there a way to avoid part of this $320,000 in tax on an estate of $1,400,000? The answer is yes. Monte can say "Thank you, but no thank you" to the property that would pass to him from his wife. The $600,000 could go to a trust that would provide him with all the income. The $600,000 owned by Anne becomes subject to tax, but the tax on $600,000 is zero because of her equivalent exemption. The amount which is sheltered could be worth even more depending on her year of death.

When Monte dies, how much does he own? Just his own $800,000. The tax on his $800,000 is $75,000, maybe less. Since Anne's estate paid no tax and Monte's estate paid just $75,000, Monte and Anne's family saved $245,000 in estate taxes because of a disclaimer.

Simultaneous Death

People frequently think about simultaneous death: "What happens if we're both killed in a plane crash?" The good news is that in over 30 years of practicing law in the estate planning area, I have seen relatively few true common disasters. Few couples die at the same time. Nevertheless, it is an area where there is considerable confusion.

The state of Florida has adopted a law entitled The Uniform Simultaneous Death Law. In essence, this law says "If two people are killed simultaneously or so close to each other that no one can tell who dies first, the law says that neither of them will inherit from the other." The next question then becomes, "What about joint property?" Here again, logic prevails. The joint property of the husband and wife is divided down the middle. One-half goes under his will and one-half goes under her will. If they have common beneficiaries, so much the better. If they do not have common beneficiaries, then one-half of her property will go to those beneficiaries under her will and one-half of his property will go to the beneficiaries under his will.

That is really all there is to the simultaneous death law. In estate planning, however, we can take advantage of other provisions in the law that are a bit more flexible and sometimes can produce some very good results. Under the federal and Florida tax law, we can provide that if a beneficiary of an estate plan survives less than 180 days the death of the person creating the estate, then the beneficiary shall be presumed to have died before the owner of the estate and will inherit nothing. Now, in fact, the beneficiary did actually survive for a while, but for the purpose of implementing the decedent's estate plan, we treat the beneficiary as if he or she died before the estate owner did. However, we are limited to just 180 days for tax purposes. It is perfectly legal to say in a will, "If any beneficiary does not survive by more than 180 days, that beneficiary shall be presumed, for the purposes of my will, to have predeceased me and shall take nothing." This becomes very useful in reducing estate taxes in some instances. If a husband and wife are involved in a car accident, and one of them dies instantly and the other dies as a result of injuries two months later, we don't have a true simultaneous death. We may have provided in the documents that the now-deceased second spouse is not to inherit anything because he or she did not survive at least 180 days.

From a practical standpoint, it is not critical to provide documents about simultaneous death. The statute is almost always going to produce the correct result—that neither of the people who died will inherit from the other.

If your attorney has not provided for a simultaneous death or for a survivorship period such as 180 days in your estate planning documents, do not be concerned. Your attorney probably has considered the effect of your assets, the simultaneous death law, and the likelihood of a simultaneous death and made a decision that it is not necessary to provide for survivorship in your will.

Summary

With a working knowledge of the federal gift tax law and the federal estate tax law and how they interrelate, we've seen how some tax wise estate planning can save considerable amounts of money. Not only annual exclusion gifts but also gifts in excess of the equivalent exemption may produce significant tax savings, especially when looking at the magic of compounding and the future growth that can occur when gifts are made.

Gifting of property that has a high basis is usually a good idea, particularly if there is some additional growth potential in these assets. Gifting of life insurance is an area that has some catches to it. Since the life insurance may well be taxable, we have to be particularly careful about the three-year rule: if the gift was made within three years prior to death, gifts of life insurance are going to be included in the giver's estate even if the giver no longer owns the property.

Splitting property between a husband and wife can be useful, particularly if it is desirable to take full advantage of each of their equivalent exemptions. Having all the property joint may cause no tax to arise upon the death of the first spouse. However, all the joint property will be included on the death of the second spouse. The result is that if the second spouse has an estate of more than the exempt amount because of the joint property, there's going to be some tax to pay which otherwise would not have arisen if some careful tax planning had taken place before the joint property tax trap had been sprung.

All in all, the basic concepts of the estate and gift tax laws are not excessively complicated. It's the exceptions, the exceptions to the exceptions, and the strange constructions that make it seem so hard. Armed with these few basic concepts, it is frequently possible to look at an estate and save considerable taxes for the ultimate beneficiaries.

In this chapter, you will learn about:

- the Uniform Transfers to Minors Act
- income and estate tax
- trusts for younger beneficiaries
- the Section 2503(c) trust
- the Section 2503(c) trust after age 21
- the Section 2503(b) trust
- mandatory income distribution
- the Crummey trust

11

GIFTS TO MINORS

We have talked about what to give, how not to give, how the gift tax works, and a number of giving techniques. Let's explore how gifts can be made to minors. If you are the impatient type, you can turn to Appendix I in the back of the book and see a table that summarizes advantages and disadvantages of the various ways of making gifts to minors. It would be better, however, to read on first and turn to the appendix later. Gifting to young people is an area of some confusion. The problems arising from improper gifts to young people can be both practical and financial. There are many ways to give property to minors. We're going to explore some of the best ways, starting off with the simplest and winding up with some of the more complex trust type of gifts.

Gifts to children and grandchildren can be most satisfying and, from a financial point of view, extremely productive. The gift has a chance to compound, and as we have seen earlier, as it compounds it becomes more and more valuable. The gift is also out of the taxable estate and thus avoids estate tax, and you have the pleasure of seeing the beneficiary enjoy the gift. When it comes to minors, things get a bit more difficult. After all, you can't give a minor $10,000 without running into pretty serious snags. Under Florida law, the child's parents as natural guardians have the right to handle up to $5,000 of the child's money. Once it gets above

$5,000, however, there must be a court-appointed legal guardianship. Court-appointed legal guardianships can be clumsy and expensive. For this reason, modest gifts to a child or grandchild who is a minor may be a good idea, but once the $5,000 threshold has been passed, it is necessary to look at alternatives.

The Uniform Transfer to Minors Act

Florida has adopted an updated version of a uniform law providing for transfers to minors. This law provides that a person will hold the gifted asset for the minor beneficiary as a custodian. This is not as a legal guardian or as a natural guardian or as a trustee in the strict sense of the word. A custodian is given certain flexibility and powers that legal guardians do not have. Gifted assets pass to the minor beneficiary when the minor reaches the age of 21. The assets are registered in the name of the individual who serves as custodian under the Florida Uniform Transfers to Minors Act. This arrangement avoids the red tape of the guardianship. It is frequently used for the transfer of stocks and bonds. In fact, if you look at the back of most stock transfer certificates, there is a legend for the transfer under either the Uniform Transfers to Minors Act or the Uniform Gifts to Minors Act.

Income and Estate Tax

Income earned in the custodial account is taxed to the child. Because of the so-called "kiddie tax" (see Chapter 7), the tax rate for children under the age of 14 is the same as their parents' rate. Once the child turns 14, the tax rate is at the child's rate, but the income is still taxed to the child. For estate tax purposes, the child is considered to be the owner of the property, and the asset will be included in the child's estate. If the custodian dies, the property is not included in the custodian's estate unless the custodian was also the giver.

If a person makes a gift under the Florida Transfers to Minors Act and names himself or herself as a custodian for the property, the Internal Revenue Service will cause the gifted property to be in the custodian's estate. The reason is that the giver still retained rights over the property that permitted the giver to determine the beneficial enjoyment of the property; in other words, it was a gift with a string attached to it. If you might have to pay estate taxes, do not name yourself as custodian of a gift you make to a minor.

Remember, there is no requirement that the gift be made at least three years before death in order to avoid having it included in the giver's estate (with the two exceptions of life insurance and the technical relinquishments of certain rights in trusts). Since the giver (donor) cannot be the custodian, sometimes the spouse is named as a custodian so that the giver can argue that the gift should not be included in the giver's estate. This may work if the spouse is not also the parent of the child who is the beneficiary of the gift.

In instances where the parent is the custodian of a minor beneficiary, the IRS has argued that the parent has a legal duty to support the minor, and the property could be included in the giver's estate. While this argument may or may not prevail, it is frequently desirable to name a trustworthy uncle or aunt of the minor. In this way, the problem of the legal duties of support and the unforeseen inclusion of the child's property in the custodian's estate is avoided.

Trust for Younger Beneficiaries

Having explored outright gifts which, if in excess of $5,000, may cause a legal guardianship to arise, we now turn to two types of trusts that are often used because of their flexibility. The first takes its name from the Internal Revenue Code Section 2503(c).

Section 2503(c) Trust

You will recall that a gift must be one of a present interest to qualify for the $10,000 annual exclusion. There is an exception to this when it comes to younger beneficiaries. The exception is found in Section 2503(c) of the Internal Revenue Code. In the case of beneficiaries under age 21, a gift may qualify for the annual exclusion as a present interest if the property can be used for the benefit of the beneficiary before attaining age 21 and if, to the extent that the gift is not consumed, it will be distributed to the beneficiary at age 21. If the beneficiary dies before reaching age 21, the property in the trust may be distributed to the beneficiary's estate. By taking advantage of this portion of the law, a trust can be set up which provides that the income and, if necessary, principal can be used for the minor beneficiary's health, support, maintenance, education, or any other good purpose that you, as the creator of the trust, wish to direct the trustee to consider at the time the trust is created.

You can name the trustee and set forth what specific powers the trustee will have and other important conditions that you feel should be included in the trust. Each year you can put up to $10,000 adjusted for inflation in the trust. Other people, should they wish, can add their $10,000 per year to this trust. The income probably will not be used and will accumulate. You know who the trustee is because you're the person who created the trust and named the trustee. Once the trust is set up, it is not necessary to do a trust each year. By the time the minor is 21, a considerable sum of money may have been accumulated. In fact, if you were to put aside $10,000 in the year a child is born and each year thereafter, and have that gifted money compound at the rate of 7% after the payment of all taxes, that $10,000 would grow to more than $400,000 upon the child's 21st birthday. Setting aside money for a young child clearly has great benefits. The 2503(c) trust provides an easy way to do this if a custodian or guardianship will not be used.

Section 2503(c) Trust After Age 21

Usually, someone will look at the amount of money that is going to pass to the beneficiary at age 21 and say "That's too much money to give a young person." Frequently it is. To deal with this problem, we have to be creative. One way is to provide that the trust will comply with the restrictions imposed by 2503(c) and that the trust will become available to the beneficiary at age 21, and to further provide that, if the child does not take the money out during a reasonable period after reaching age 21 (say, 60 days), the trust then becomes irrevocable. This means the assets in the trust are now protected against possible spendthrift tendencies of a young person, and the money can stay in the trust.

The child must have the right to take out the principal without any restrictions after age 21. But after that, the trust can provide that if the child does not take out the funds, then only the income is used for the child's benefit. The principal stays there and is not distributed to the child until perhaps ages 25, 30, and 35. In fact, it is not even a requirement that the income be distributed after a child turns 21 and the 60-day time period has passed. However, many people would prefer to have the income distributed to the child by this time in order to give the child some experience in receiving and handling money.

If substantial sums of money are to be set aside, the 2503(c) trust should be considered. There is flexibility in creating the trust document in that it can be crafted, shaped, and molded according to your wishes. Subject only to the requirements of 2503(c), the trust can receive large sums of money, invest them, see them grow, and, upon the child's 21st birthday, acknowledge the child's right to the funds. Typically, the child does not exercise the right to take the funds out. Thereafter, the trust continues to grow and provide income and, if necessary, principal when a child is getting married, buying a home, or having children.

Section 2503(b) Trust

We saw that the guardianship or custodianship has a disadvantage in that assets go to the beneficiary at age 21. We also saw that the 2503(c) trust had an advantage in that the trust could be shaped as you wished and that if the funds were not taken out after a child turned 21, the trust could continue. Some beneficiaries, however, might exercise their right to take the principal out. To be certain that this will not happen, a 2503(b) trust is set up. The 2503(b) trust, or current income trust, is a hybrid type of trust. It provides assurance that the principal will not go to the beneficiary when he or she turns 21. This trust, however, requires the giver to give up certain tax benefits.

Mandatory Income Distribution

The Section 2503(b) trust requires a mandatory distribution of all income received by this trust. The way this trust works is a bit complex.

What happens is that the entire property transferred to the trust is considered to be a gift, but then that gift is considered to have two components—the income portion and the principal portion. Since the income must be distributed to the beneficiary, the income portion qualifies as a present interest for the annual exclusion. The other portion (the principal portion) does not qualify for the annual exclusion and is required to be reported on a federal gift tax return. The allocation between the principal and income is made based upon IRS tables. These tables change frequently because the "deemed rate of return" depends upon the interest rates charged in the financial world.

The 2503(b) trust has the advantage that the principal may not be taken out by the beneficiary at age 21. In fact, the principal may never be distributed to the beneficiary if that is what the trust provides. This trust is the most complex of the types of trusts typically used for gifts to minors. Many people who want to make substantial gifts to minors prefer to use the 2503(c) trust because it's easy to set up and because they hope and expect that the beneficiary will not exercise the right to take the funds out upon reaching age 21. Nevertheless, the 2503(b) trust does have an important advantage since the principal does not go to the beneficiary at age 21.

Crummey Trust

One of the most used trusts bears a very unimposing name—the Crummey trust. This trust takes advantage of the provisions in the Internal Revenue Code by permitting a person to make annual gifts of $10,000 a year and by recognizing the necessity that these gifts will be gifts of a present interest.

How can we couple these ideas together with a trust so as to provide a very useful vehicle in making gifts for the benefit of young people? We can create an irrevocable trust which says that gifts may be distributed to the trustee. Each year the trustee, upon receiving the gift, shall notify the beneficiary that the beneficiary has a reasonable period of time—say, 30 to 45 days—in which to take the asset out. If the beneficiary chooses not to take the money out, then the gift stays in the trust and the beneficiary cannot take the money out later if he or she changes his or her mind.

What has happened is that we have made a gift of a present interest because the beneficiary had the right to take the money out for a reasonable period of time but simply chose not to. If the money is left in, the trust gift should qualify for the annual exclusion as a gift of a present interest. At the same time, we know that the beneficiary cannot take the money out later because that right has been given up.

Let's see how this works in practice. Joe has two daughters. He wants to set aside some extra money for their benefit, but he does not want them to have the money when they turn 21. He is hopeful that there will be a considerable sum of money in the trust. He has thought about a 2503(c) trust, but doesn't want to take the risk that either of the girls might decide to take the money out at age 21. Even if they have only 60 days to think about it, one might decide in that time that she really would like to have a red Corvette.

Accordingly, Joe decides to set up a Crummey trust. He is thinking about an irrevocable trust and wants to name his brother, Ben, as trustee. Ben would be authorized to distribute as much income or principal as he deems fit for the girls' health, support, maintenance, or education.

Recognizing that it is possible that one of the girls might have more needs than the other, he decides to set up two separate trusts, one for Beth and one for Debbie. That way if Ben, as trustee, decides to take out some money for one of the girls, the other girl won't be penalized. Each trust says that the income will start going to Beth or Debbie at age 21. Distributions of principal will occur with one-third going to each daughter from her own trust when she turns 25, one-third at 30, and the balance of the trust at 35.

So far, the trust sounds perfect. However, we have not yet dealt with the question of how to make this a present interest gift. Joe provides in the trust agreement that at any time his brother receives some funds to put in the trust, he is to advise Debbie or Beth that funds have come into her particular trust. Debbie or Beth would have 45 days to direct Ben to distribute the newly added trust funds to her.

Note here that neither Debbie or Beth has the right to take out all the

spouse. In this way, the couple can take advantage of the estate tax exemption which the poorer spouse has as well. While the actual tax savings may vary depending on the total amount of assets and the tax brackets, between $200,000 and $300,000 in estate taxes can be saved by putting more assets in the poorer spouse's name (see Appendix J).

Let's suppose that Ted and Sally are a happily married couple and that the marriage has been of some duration. Ted has all the assets—approximately $1,300,000—in his name. If Sally dies first, there will be no way to use her estate tax exemption in her estate. After all, she did not have any assets in her name. Her estate tax exemption will be lost. Let's look at the tax effect. When Ted dies, his estate, valued at approximately $1,300,000, could have a tax bite around $258,500. On the other hand, if they had split up their assets so that Ted had half and Sally had half, the tax bite on Sally's death would have been zero, because she would have been able to use her estate tax exemption. The tax bite on Ted's death would also have been zero because he would also have had his exemption. They would have avoided the tax and their children would have received that much more from the estate.

Restrictions on the Marital Deduction

In order for assets passing to a surviving spouse to qualify for the marital deduction, the law does impose some certain, reasonable limitations or restrictions on how these assets can pass. The first of these is that the assets must pass to a spouse. It is necessary that the couple have entered into a valid marriage. Persons in a same-sex relationship will not be entitled to the marital deduction. Similarly, persons who may have lived together for an extended period of time, and in fact may have lived together as husband and wife to the world, would not be entitled to the marital deduction if they have not entered into a valid marriage either at law or common law. (The number of common law marriages existing in the state of Florida is small and decreasing since new common law marriages have not been recognized by Florida for many years. A common law marriage is created when a man and woman present themselves to the community as husband and wife for an extended period of time.)

Citizenship

Another limitation which the tax law imposes is a requirement that the surviving spouse be a citizen of the United States. This has become increasingly important as Florida has received many visitors from outside the United States, some of whom have decided to make their homes, or at least purchase real estate, here. Florida has many Canadians as well as people from France, Germany, and other European countries who, while owning property in the state of Florida, are not entitled to the marital deduction.

An exception to this limitation was written into the tax law. This exception provides that a spouse who is not a United States citizen may take action to enable assets to qualify for the marital deduction. This is done by placing the assets in certain types of trusts which will provide assurance to the United States government that when the non-United States citizen spouse dies, the assets are subject to taxation by the United States. This recent change in the tax law was enacted in order to prevent assets that were not taxed upon the death of the first spouse from being exported to the surviving spouse's home country, resulting in the United States government's not being able to tax those assets on the death of the second spouse either.

If we have a valid marriage to a person who is a United States citizen, then the qualification of the marital deduction is rather easy. All that is necessary to qualify for the marital deduction is simply to pass assets to the surviving spouse. Where we run into trouble occasionally is when people start putting limitations or qualifications on the property passing to the surviving spouse.

The No-Strings Transfer

The no-strings transfer will always qualify for the marital deduction, but once strings are put on a transfer, the likelihood is that the marital deduction is going to be lost. A transfer to a husband or a wife with, for example, the proviso that if either he or she were to remarry, the property would go to the couple's children, will cause the property passing to that surviving spouse to not qualify for the marital deduction. Therefore, it is usually not a good idea to place strings on the marital deduction. There is, however, one type of marital deduction string which is frequently used and which will not cause the marital deduction to the estate of the first spouse to be jeopardized.

QTIP Marital Deduction

The QTIP marital deduction, more formally known as *Qualified Terminable Interest Property*, responds to the wishes of many married people to provide for their spouses, yet, at the same time, to have assurance that the property, upon the death of the second spouse, will pass to the designated beneficiaries, such as the first spouse's children. We see this type of marital deduction frequently in second marriages but also occasionally in first marriages. Since it offers some attractive estate planning opportunities, let us take a look in some detail at this unusual type of marital deduction.

Essentially, the QTIP marital deduction is property which is placed in trust for the benefit of the surviving spouse on the death of the first spouse. Under the terms of the trust, provision is made that the surviving spouse will receive all the income from the property in the trust. No qualifications or strings are attached on the right to get the income. The principal, however, may be—but need not be—available to the surviving spouse, unlike the traditional marital deduction where the surviving spouse has the right to receive the income *plus* as much of the principal as he or she wishes.

Here, the principal is usually set aside for the next group of beneficiaries. Frequently, provisions are made that permit the principal to be invaded by the trustee for the surviving spouse's health or support, but this provision is not necessary. What is necessary, however, is that the surviving spouse must have the absolute, unrestricted right to receive all the income for life. If this is done and the principal is set aside so that it can never be invaded during the spouse's lifetime for anyone other than the spouse (if at all), then the property will qualify for the QTIP.

Now it is easy to see why this is such a popular item. After all, in second marriages, many people want to provide for their spouses. They love them very much, but at the same time, they want to be assured that when they die, their property will go to their children and that their spouses will not give it away to new spouses or to their own children.

By using the advantages of a QTIP, a husband and wife can set up a trust in the estate plan. That trust will provide that the spouse will receive all the income for as long as the spouse is alive. Further, as noted above, the principal may or may not be invaded for the benefit of the surviving spouse, depending upon the terms of the agreement itself. This provides assurance to the first spouse that when he or she dies, the other spouse will be provided for. On the other hand, the first spouse also knows that the property he or she worked so hard for or which he or she may have inherited from a former spouse will in fact go to the children of the first marriage or at least will not be unwisely spent by the surviving spouse.

While we have been considering the marital deduction and the QTIP in the context of a second marriage, the QTIP is also frequently used in estate planning for couples who have been married many years and who have children only by that marriage. Sometimes, one spouse feels that the other spouse should not be burdened with the responsibility of managing the money. Sometimes, both spouses agree that the surviving spouse should not be subjected to the requests of children importuning the surviving spouse, perhaps now in declining health, to give them money out of the marital trust. By explaining to the children that the surviving spouse has only the income interest and does not have the ability to invade the principal, the widow or widower will be able to tell the children clearly that he or she cannot invade the trust and therefore cannot give money to one or more of the children.

Finally, there is a subject that not many people talk about, but it is one that comes up in the minds of many persons considering estate planning, particularly those with a number of years of experience. What if the surviving spouse becomes burdened with years of living? Old age or infirmity creeps in and the discretion to invade is exercised unwisely. By being able to invade the principal, they make themselves vulnerable to fortune seekers, to marriages late in life in which the younger spouse makes demands for money, or simply to poor investments as a result of high-pressure salesmen. All these considerations are very valid and very human reasons for creating the QTIP marital deduction. The QTIP provides the surviving spouse with a steady income stream from the assets in the trust, but at the same time provides all parties concerned with assurance that the assets in this trust will pass to the designated beneficiaries. The surviving spouse cannot invade the principal of this trust and cannot will the principal of this trust to persons other than those designated.

The Limited Power of Appointment of the QTIP—A Second Look

Occasionally, we use a variation of the QTIP. Here, the trust is set up with the income going to the surviving spouse. The principal may be invaded by the trustee only for the benefit of the surviving spouse in limited circumstances. Here, however, the surviving spouse is given what is called a limited power of appointment. This provides that the surviving spouse, in his or her will, can direct to whom the principal in the marital QTIP trust will be distributed when he or she dies. However, this discretion as to who will receive the principal in the marital QTIP trust is limited to a class of beneficiaries. Typically, those beneficiaries are lineal descendants of the first spouse.

Why would you want to make this kind of provision? Sometimes, there is a significant change in the family after the death of the first spouse. If the first spouse's estate plan directs that all the principal in the marital QTIP trust will go equally to the children, then that's exactly what will happen. However, by giving the surviving spouse, who is the income beneficiary of the QTIP trust, the power to redirect the property among the children and grandchildren, we have given this surviving spouse a "second look." By giving the spouse a second look, we have provided flexibility that may be very desirable if circumstances change. One of the children could develop a significant medical problem, for instance, and may need more assets than the other children. With a second look, the surviving spouse can then redirect more of that principal to the child in need.

Sometimes, a child may be very successful financially and have little or no desire for additional funds. Here, funds can be directed away from that child. Conversely, a child may demonstrate a total inability to handle funds. Here again, funds can be directed away from that child and over to the other children or a trustee for the benefit of that spendthrift child. By using the flexibility of the second look, yet, at the same time, having the absolute certainty that the property will not go to any group other than lineal descendants, estate planners can provide a very desirable mix of certainty and flexibility.

The ability to freely transfer property between spouses, either during lifetime or on death, is of great importance. This unlimited right to transfer assets to the spouse is important not only because it provides opportunities for estate planning, but also because it provides assurance to the surviving spouse when the estate plan is in place that neither he nor she will be deprived because of some provisions in the estate law. Because of the unlimited transfer of assets, we no longer have to deal with this problem.

While such was not always the case, for today and probably for at least the foreseeable future, there is the unlimited right to transfer assets tax free to a spouse. After all, while we see the tremendous number of changes that occur each year in the tax law, such a fundamental change would have far-reaching impact, both economically and politically. Few politicians are brave enough to stand up and tell the American public that they are going to vote for a law which will tax your assets when you give them to your husband or wife.

In this chapter, you will learn:

- why the durable power of attorney is important
- whether you need a living will
- whether a trust is right for you
- how to make an estate plan
- whether annuities are right for you
- how to arrange for management of the estate
- what prenuptial and postnuptial agreements contain
- what a forced share is
- whether you need specialized estate planning

13

ESTATE PLANNING FOR THE SINGLE PERSON

Let's face it: Being single can be difficult in many ways—loneliness, a lack of companionship, a lack of someone with whom to share. There is also often the lack of a support system—someone not only with whom to talk and share things, but also someone who is there when needed. Being single is also difficult for estate planning.

The estate tax law provides many benefits, such as marital deductions, for people who are married, yet it is true that most people die single. After all, even if almost everyone married and never divorced, 50% of the people would die married and 50% would die single. There are large numbers of people who are not married and, therefore, most people will go through some period in their adult lives when they are single. For many of these people, this period will occur toward the end of their lives, when they are thinking about estate planning.

Durable Power of Attorney

Some of the first things that a single person should consider are, How are my affairs going to be managed if I am unable to manage them? Who is going to make the decisions, and what authority should he or she have? What guidance will be given in making those decisions? These are important questions, many of which were discussed in Chapter 3.

Under Florida law, a person is permitted to make out a durable power of attorney. (A typical durable power of attorney is included in Appendix D.) It is extremely broad in what it covers, and it should be. The durable power of attorney is intended to provide for guidance and authority in managing a person's affairs if he or she is unable to do so.

The durable power of attorney is particularly helpful for the single person. It gives the single person some assurance as to who is going to manage his or her affairs. It also gives the appointed person a broad authority to manage the single person's affairs. The durable power of attorney should be as broad as possible, since people have many types of assets.

The power of attorney should always be executed before it is actually needed. By that time, in many instances, it is already too late. A person who, through illness or misfortune, has lost the ability to manage his or her affairs may also be unable to sign and give the durable power of attorney at that critical time.

Sometimes, the durable power of attorney is used in instances when the person who is giving the power of attorney is just going to be out of touch for a period of time. Perhaps he or she is taking a trip abroad for a month and wants to be sure someone will be available to take care of things. In this instance, of course, "take care of things" means much more than taking in the mail and looking after the house or condominium. It means, perhaps, answering questions and in some instances making financial decisions. So, durable powers of attorney are used in two instances: They cover the situation in which a person has become incapacitated and unable to manage financial affairs, and they also cover the times when, by reason of temporary illness or absence, a person is not able to effectively handle things and wishes someone else to take over for a relatively brief period.

The durable power of attorney is always completely revocable. If for some reason you feel the holder might exercise the power in ways you wish he or she would not, you can cancel it.

Living Wills and Health Care Surrogates

Living wills and health care surrogates are especially important for single people. Although these subjects were covered in Chapter 4, we'll summarize briefly. Living wills provide instructions to health care providers in the event a person has a terminal illness and death is imminent. Health care surrogates provide someone to make decisions if a person is unable to make his or her own medical decisions. Florida law is not fixed in this area. It seems to be moving in the direction of giving greater latitude to people who want to provide instructions for their medical care.

The single person does not have a spouse to make health care decisions for him or her. A family member, such as a child or sibling, certainly can do this, but having the living will and health care surrogate document gives that person a great deal of legal and emotional assurance as to what steps should be taken and what instructions are to be given. It is more important for a single person to have a living will and a health care surrogate than for a married person to have one. The married couple may well have spent some time discussing what they would like to do and what approaches they would like taken, so that each knows the other's wishes through this time of sharing. With the single person, this may not have occurred with a sibling or a child or may not have occurred in a long time.

The durable power of attorney, the health care surrogate, and living will form a natural trio of documents that the single person should consider.

Trusts

Trusts are also important to the single person. The trust can be a living or *inter vivos* trust, or can be set up in a will.

For the single person who is over 65, a living trust may be desirable. Of course, it is not going to be possible to have your assets joint with your spouse if you are single. By having the assets set up in a living trust, you have already designated who is to manage the assets and who will inherit them. You have given the person who is acting as trustee—which may be yourself initially and then your successor trustee—broad authority in managing these assets.

The Single Person's Estate Plan

The durable power of attorney, the living will, the health care surrogate, and the will or living trust are the most important documents for the single person. Once these are in place, we should look at the estate plan itself. One of the most important aspects of the estate plan is that there is no marital deduction. We saw in the preceding chapters that the marital deduction provided for the greatest estate tax savings. With the single person, estate taxes become much more significant. Since deferral is no longer possible through the marital deduction, we need to look at other tax savings possibilities.

Annuities

Annuities have considerable advantages for single people. One advantage is that they provide a guaranteed income for life. This income is greater than investments such as stocks, bonds, or certificates of deposit (CDs) because the annuity ends on the death of the single person. The single person may not be seeking to leave a large estate and may well appreciate the high income stream that the annuity provides. This income is significantly increased over the income that would be recognized solely from the income on investments without a partial return of capital. The single person also appreciates the security of an annuity issued by a large financial institution with very high ratings. It is essential that the issuer of the annuity be among the most highly rated by the companies that rate financial providers of annuities. After all, when you're alone, there's no one to fall back on. There's no safety net. As a single person, you must be conservative in many of your approaches to financial planning. The best investment might not be the one with the greatest yield, but rather the one with the most certain yield.

Prenuptial and Postnuptial Agreements in Florida

One of the things about being single is that you can still get married. For the single Floridian, getting married significantly affects estate planning.

We will now cover the more important aspects of estate planning for the single person who is contemplating marriage. If a marriage occurs later in life, particularly when there are children from a prior marriage, the question of a prenuptial or postnuptial agreement frequently comes up.

Prenuptial Agreements

Prenuptial agreements are agreements on property rights entered into before marriage. Prenuptial agreements are favored under the laws of Florida because they set forth what the parties wish to have done with their assets. Each party to the marriage is assured that his or her assets will not be taken if he or she dies first. Assets can be set aside for children or loved ones without the possibility of a forced sharing with a spouse under Florida law.

Postnuptial Agreements

Postnuptial agreements, like their name implies, are agreements on property rights between spouses entered into after marriage. Unlike prenuptial agreements, postnuptial agreements are reviewed very carefully by the courts. The concern here is that, subsequent to marriage, one of the parties may exercise undue influence or apply pressure on the other spouse to cause him or her to give up property rights.

It is essential that each spouse carefully identifies goals, that each has the opportunity to consult with his or her own personal attorney, and that all assets are carefully spelled out and disclosed to the other spouse. Because the opportunity for pressure by one spouse on the other is so great, each spouse should have an attorney. The postnuptial agreement can correct oversights or address questions that have come up because of a change in circumstance. Sometimes people want to get married and do not want to think about the financial aspects of their union. Therefore, they will marry and only later begin to consider items such as property rights. Postnuptial agreements function very much like prenuptial agreements. They set forth the financial understandings between the parties and give husband and wife the assurance that their assets will go to their designated beneficiaries upon the death of one of them.

The Elective or Forced Share

Florida law provides that the household goods up to a value of $10,000, together with any automobile that had been used by the decedent, as well as 30% of the assets passing through probate, may be chosen by the surviving spouse regardless of what the will says. The spouse can do this against the will of the deceased spouse simply by filing an election. This is sometimes known as a forced share or elective share, and is similar to the earlier concepts of dower or curtesy.

Many people who marry agree with each other that they will not do this, and they sign a prenuptial agreement. The agreement also says that neither will seek any alimony or support from the other. Each agrees that they will not make any claims against the other's estate. Each, however, is free to provide as much as he or she wishes for the surviving spouse. There certainly is no language in the agreement prohibiting a spouse from leaving his or her estate, or any portion of the estate, to the surviving spouse, but neither is *required* to do so.

Joint property would pass to the surviving spouse and would not be adversely affected by the prenuptial agreement. It is important when considering a prenuptial agreement, however, to read the documents carefully. Not all prenuptial agreements say the same thing. Also, there may be provisions in the prenuptial agreement for the husband or wife in the event there is a dissolution of the marriage. Divorces do occur and people need to know what they can and cannot do and what the courts do in the event that this happens.

Generally speaking, it is desirable to incorporate in the prenuptial agreement a financial statement from each of the persons signing the prenuptial agreement. For estate planning purposes, Florida law does not require this for prenuptial agreements, although it does require it for postnuptial agreements. Careful practitioners, however, do incorporate financial statements for each of the spouses as a safety precaution. The attorney may also check to see if the client owns any real estate in a state other than Florida. The prenuptial agreement will be applicable to all Florida assets.

Whether it is applicable to assets such as real estate owned outside the state will depend on where the real estate is located. Some states favor prenuptial agreements; others do not. A typical prenuptial agreement is attached as Appendix K.

Estate Planning

Estate planning is challenging for the single person. It is difficult, but there are no insurmountable problems. It just takes a little more time, thought, and effort. There is also the satisfaction of knowing that you are doing things on your own; you are the captain of your own ship. There is a certain amount of pride in knowing that you *can* do it and are doing it, whether you are a young person who does not expect to marry or a person who has been married and is now single. Whatever these difficult times might be, you are learning and beginning to do things. The fact that you are reading this book in itself speaks of who you are and what you have been able to accomplish so far.

As a single person, you have some tools to meet these challenges. First, you have the durable power of attorney with which you can give someone control over your financial affairs. Second, you have the health care surrogate designation, a power of attorney for health care. It provides guidance and legal authority to the person whom you name as your health care surrogate, giving him or her specific rights and responsibilities in dealing with your health care matters. Physicians, hospitals, nursing homes, and other health care providers will be much more responsive to someone you have named as your health care surrogate. Third, you have the living will which gives instructions concerning your medical care decisions when you are terminally ill and death is imminent, or if you are in a persistent vegetative state. Finally, you have trusts, those flexible devices that permit you to designate who is to manage your financial affairs if for some reason you are unable to do so. There are almost no limitations as to who can be a trustee, so the flexibility and field of choices is quite broad.

Give some thought to the management of your property while you are alive and its distribution to your beneficiaries upon death. You will see that estate planning for the single person is, in the final analysis, not really that much different than estate planning for other persons.

In this chapter, you will learn:

- the importance of knowing your charity
- what is deductible
- what the charitable deduction is
- what substantiation and overvaluation mean
- what to consider in estate planning
- what charitable remainder trusts are
- what a pooled income fund is
- how to give gifts of tangible personal property
- what a charitable residence gift is
- whether to give life insurance
- what a charitable lead trust is

14

CHARITABLE GIVING

As a long and honored tradition in estate planning, charitable giving is well established. Indeed, the gifts of individuals and corporations to charities have made our society a substantially better one than it otherwise would be.

The role of charitable giving in the estate planning area is recognized in the Internal Revenue Code and by careful practitioners as a useful adjunct to formulating a good overall estate plan. While it is generally not really possible to "make money by giving it away," there are a number of techniques that can be used advantageously to provide the best possible result in making charitable gifts. It will be the best result both in the sense of maximizing financial return and in the sense of being most productive in a practical and a charitable sense.

We'll look at some of the ways charitable giving works from an estate planning standpoint regarding both income tax and estate tax. Then we'll move into some of the more complex and interesting possibilities of charitable giving.

Know Your Charity

First, let's look at income tax and charitable contributions. The first rule is to know your charity. Charities come in many varieties—some good and some not so good. Some may not even be recognized as charities by the Internal Revenue Service.

The best way to get to know your charity from a tax standpoint is to ask the charity for a copy of its tax determination letter. Any charity should be able to give you this unless it is the type of organization that is not required to have such a letter, such as churches and temples which, by their nature, are recognized as being charitable. Many do not ask for or receive tax determination letters from the IRS.

Deductibility

The IRS assigns two levels of deductibility for charitable contributions. It imposes a maximum on the amount given to all charities cumulatively. You can give up to 50% of your adjusted gross income to public charities and get a full deduction for the contributions. These are called "50% charities." In the case of nonpublic charities—that is, private and semipublic charities—the maximum that can be deducted is 30% of your adjusted gross income. Fifty-percent charities are those that we typically recognize as being charities: medical research organizations, governments, schools, hospitals, churches, temples, and universities. All these are recognized by the IRS as tax-deductible charities. The 30% semipublic and private charities are more likely to be organizations such as nonprofit cemetery associations, private foundations, veteran's organizations, and fraternal organizations that operate under a lodge system.

If you give to a bona fide charity recognized by the IRS as a charitable organization, how much is your deduction?

What Is the Deduction?

A taxpayer is allowed a 100% deduction for property contributed to a charity. The amount of the deduction is almost always the fair market value of the property at the time of the contribution. Cash is the easiest thing in the world to value. Gifts of stocks and bonds that are traded on a major exchange have a readily determined value, which is the value the security had when it was transferred to the charity.

Substantiation and Overvaluation

There have been some problems over the years with people who inflated the values of gifts to charities. This problem became almost epidemic several years ago. There was a cottage industry of unscrupulous individuals who would sell you assets cheaply with the idea that part of their product would be a highly inflated appraisal. You could attach this appraisal to your tax return, substantiating a very generous donation to the charity. The sellers claimed you would actually make more money than the cost of the goods. Obviously, this was a violation of both the spirit and the letter of the law. It resulted in new regulations requiring substantiation of the gifts of tangible property. The substantiation is required for gifts of more than $5,000 fair market value. An appraisal must be attached to the tax return setting forth the appraiser's qualifications and asserting that the appraiser has no relationship with the giver of the property.

The IRS, however, went further and set a substantial penalty for significant overvaluation. A penalty of 30% of the tax that was not paid applies if property is overvalued by 150% of its final fair market value. Thus, if an item were listed as a $7,500 charitable gift and in fact its value was $4,000, the overvaluation would be more than 150% and the penalty would be 30% of the tax saved. This is not the end of the story. The IRS may also charge a penalty for negligence. Thus, the scam of significantly overvaluing gifts to charities was ended for all but the most naive.

Loss Property

Loss property is property with a basis higher than its current market value. It is not a good idea to give this kind of property to charities. The maximum charitable deduction is the fair market value rather than your higher basis. Because of this, it is wiser to sell the property. Establish the loss for tax purposes; lock in the loss on your personal tax return, and then give the net proceeds to the charity and take a charitable deduction for this. In this way, you get *both* the deduction of the amount given to charity and the tax loss when you sold at a loss. If you just give it to the charity, you lose the benefit of your tax loss.

Estate Planning Aspects

Having looked at the income tax aspects of charitable giving briefly, let's turn to the estate planning aspects of charitable giving. They are similar to the income tax rules for charitable giving, but there are some significant differences.

Making a Charitable Gift and Keeping the Income

Making a charitable gift, removing the asset from being taxed in your estate, and keeping the income sounds too good to be true. But there are some very real, legitimate tax breaks that can be used through sophisticated estate planning and gifts to charities.

Gifts to charities can be made through what are called charitable remainder trusts. There are two types of these trusts: the annuity trust and the unitrust. Both will be discussed in detail shortly. In general, however, the way these trusts work is simple in concept, although in day-to-day practice, it can get rather complex. Basically, you set aside some money in an *irrevocable* trust. You provide in the trust that you will receive distribution based on a designated percentage of principal each year. This may be 7%, 8%, or whatever seems best for you, subject to a few limitations. The distribution is made first from income the trust earns. Upon your death, whatever is left in the trust then goes to the charity. This way, you receive the designated percentage of the trust, like income, yet you also have the property out of your estate. As an added benefit, you also get a substantial income tax deduction when the trust is set up.

Annuity Trust

The annuity trust is a type of charitable remainder trust that functions as an annuity, hence its name. The annuity trust is irrevocable. Funds are put into the trust, and the income is measured by the value of the trust times the percentage chosen when the trust is created. If you create a charitable annuity trust with $100,000 in it and specify that you receive 10%, the $10,000 per year would be distributed each year until death. The value of the trust may go up or down, but the distribution is always $10,000 per year.

Income Tax on Funds Received from the Trust

The value of the charitable gift is the value of the charitable trust after deducting the right to receive the income for life. The value is based on government tables which define the values of these types of gifts. The tables are generated by computer programs which integrate a number of variables in complex mathematical formulas. The variables are the rate of interest that the person is asking to be paid, his or her life expectancy, and the current rate of interest which the federal government deems a reasonable rate of return for investments having an approximate life expectancy equal to the person's life expectancy. If, for example, the government tables based on these mathematical formulas indicated that a 7% yield was appropriate based on the length of the investment and the interest rates at the time the person signed the trust, but 10% of the amount put in the trust was paid out, the IRS would consider that a charitable gift had been made, reduced to reflect the additional 3% being paid out over current interest rates.

When the $10,000 in our example is distributed to the beneficiary, it is first considered to be ordinary taxable income to the extent that the trust has ordinary income and then capital gains. The distribution is next considered to be from tax-exempt income. If the trust has no ordinary income, no capital gains, and no tax-exempt income, only then is the distribution considered a return of principal. People frequently want to set up a charitable remainder trust that will earn tax-exempt income in the future. This way, the person not only gets an income tax deduction when the trust is set up for the charitable contribution, but also gets the money (which is received in the form of the annuity amount such as the $10,000) tax free.

It is not a good idea to specify in the trust that the trustee shall invest only in tax exempts. This violates IRS regulations. However, there is nothing which says the trustee cannot decide to invest in tax exempts. It might be that the trustee considers tax-exempt investments a wise and prudent use of the money you have contributed. The important thing is that nothing in the trust can be construed to prohibit or to require the trustee to invest in tax exempts. For estate tax purposes, if a trust ends on your death and distributes to charity, there is no estate tax on this property.

Unitrust

The companion trust to the annuity trust is the unitrust. It is similar to the annuity trust but with two differences. The unitrust is interesting because the value of the percentage of return, such as 10% in our example above, is calculated not just at the time the trust is created, but each year as well. This means that, unlike the annuity trust, if the value of the trust goes up, the actual return increases. Thus, our $100,000 trust might increase to $150,000. If this were the case, the 10% would go to $15,000 rather than just the $10,000 in the case of the annuity trust. Conversely, if you expect a recession, the annuity trust is much more desirable than the unitrust because the amount distributed is fixed at the time the trust is signed and will not go down in a recession.

The second difference is that with the unitrust, funds can be added after it is set up. Funds cannot be added to the annuity trust after it is first funded. Since the unitrust is valued each year, the added funds can be taken into account for subsequent years.

Two-Life Trusts

In the case of both annuity and unitrust documents, it is possible to use trusts which are based on not just the life of one person, but on the lifetimes of two people. For example, Linda might want to make a charitable contribution and enjoy the income tax deduction, yet retain some income interest, such as 10% on the value of the contribution each year. She might also want to provide after her death that her sister, Carol, receive the same 10% for Carol's lifetime. Setting up two-life trusts works out well. Linda receives the 10% during her lifetime and an income tax charitable deduction. On her death, the 10% continues for Carol's lifetime. Upon the death of Carol, the charity receives the money. This "two-life annuity trust" or "two-life unitrust" functions the same way as the single life trust with the exception that the income period is measured over the lives of both Linda and Carol rather than just Linda. Husbands and wives frequently set up such a trust to be sure each of them will have the income as long as either of them is alive. The deduction will be less than with a one-life trust because the period the charity must wait to get the money is longer.

The Pooled Income Fund

Another way to make a gift to charity and retain the income is through the pooled income fund. Pooled income funds are not run by small charities; they are definitely a large charity project. Here, people contribute funds to the charity, and the charity promises to pay them their proportionate amount of income earned by the pooled income fund. It is like a mutual fund run by a charity, except that it is irrevocable and the charity is the manager of the mutual fund. You, as the creator, must retain the income right for your lifetime. If you wish to add other persons, you may do so, but it must be at least for your lifetime.

If the pooled income trust fund has been in existence for more than three years, the IRS will look at the trust's performance on the income investment side. If it has been in existence less than three years, the IRS assumes a rate of return of 9%. Before making a charitable contribution to a pooled income fund, it is prudent to ask how long the trust has been in existence, what its actual yield is, and what type of investment philosophies are followed by the trustees. Since the IRS is going to assume that your rate of return was 9% for the first three years of the trust, it would be disappointing if it turned out that your income was substantially less than that.

The charitable annuity trust, the unitrust, and the pooled income fund are the three general ways in which you can give property away and still receive an income interest on it. Are there other ways to give away property and still enjoy it?

Gifts of Homes and Tangible Personal Property

A gift of tangible personal property in which you retain the right to use the property for your lifetime is not a charitable gift in the eyes of the IRS. Despite what you may have heard, a gift of tangible personal property with a retained right to use or enjoy the property will not qualify as a charitable deduction for income tax or estate tax purposes. You cannot tell the museum, for example, that you have given them a certain painting on your death, but in the meantime, you are going to keep it for your lifetime. Even if you give the museum a bill of sale or deed of gift legally establishing that they are going to get the painting on your death, this is not a charitable gift for tax purposes.

Charitable Residence Gift

There is exception to the general rule that says you have not made a charitable gift if you retain the right to use the property. The exception applies to homes and farms. If you make a legally binding transfer and retain only the right to live in the home as long as you live or for a term of years, you receive a charitable income tax deduction. The gift must be irrevocable because you are getting the deduction. Personal residence means property used for personal and not for investment purposes. It is not limited to the principal residence but includes vacation homes as well. Farms follow the same rule, even though they are not personal residences.

The Charitable Gift Annuity

Charitable gift annuities have been around for some time. They are becoming more and more popular now, principally through aggressive marketing. They work this way: Assets are transferred to the charity outright. The charity promises to pay the annuity for a lifetime or for a fixed term of years. The amount of the charitable deduction is computed based upon the charitable gift's fair market value on the date of transfer to the charity, less the value of the charity's promise to pay you income for life. The payments on the annuity can start immediately, or they can be deferred until some specified age. Interestingly enough, a portion of each annuity payment is considered nontaxable income for the recipient. Compare this to the charitable annuity trust and the charitable unitrust where all, some, or none of the income may be subject to income tax depending upon the income in the trust.

Also, it is very important to understand that the transfer of appreciated property to the charity for a charitable gift annuity may cause some tax liability to arise. After all, this is more like a sale than an outright gift. There may be some capital gains when you transfer appreciated property to the charity and receive its promise to give you money. Sometimes gift annuities are set up for a husband and wife. This, of course, reduces the value of the charitable gift because we have two lives and a longer period of time over which the charity will be paying income.

Life Insurance

Life insurance in the charitable area has also received a lot of attention recently and, in this case, the attention is justified. The amount that a charity will get through a gift of a life insurance policy can be very substantial. There is an "internal" buildup of income or value in a policy. This favorable tax treatment helps the charity receive more than if the donor just kept the policy. The charitable gift is considered to be a gift of the value of the policy at the time the policy is given. The same rules apply as in other assets. However, life insurance can be difficult for the layperson to value. A complex approach is used involving what is called the interpolated terminal reserve value. This usually translates into something like cash value. The actual figures must come from the life insurance company.

A charitable gift need not be made more than three years before death, even considering the special rules relating to the taxability of life insurance in a person's estate. When insurance is given to a charity, however, the three-year transfer rule applies but is not much of a problem. For example, if you transfer life insurance to a charity and do not live for three years, the IRS will include the value of the life insurance in your estate, but your estate gets a charitable deduction for the full value of the life insurance in your estate. What have you really lost?

Charitable Lead Trust

In the two types of charitable remainder trusts discussed above, the giver received the income and the charity received the remainder. Is it possible and is it ever desirable to reverse the pattern so that the charity gets the income for a fixed period of time and then the remainder comes back to the donor or his beneficiaries? The answer is yes.

The charitable lead trust, or front trust, provides that the charity receive a determined income for a determinable period of time. Charitable lead trusts are particularly useful for very wealthy individuals or individuals who are charitably inclined and who have a current high income but whose income may decrease substantially in the future (for example, a highly compensated executive). The trust is set up while the person is alive. The charity receives the income for a period of time. With the charitable lead trust, the wealthy person can carry out his or her charitable purposes during high-income periods and still have the assets return later, such as after retirement, when there may be more need for them.

Charitable Giving Is Not a Way to Make Money

Although charitable giving is not a way to make money, it does create significant tax breaks for the giver, and there is a very real sense of satisfaction in setting aside substantial funds for a charity in an estate plan. You may even obtain a bit of immortality through making a substantial charitable gift and having a special fund bear your name. More important is the pleasure of knowing you have done something good for society that will be of a long-term nature. How that charitable gift is set up depends on many considerations: What types of property should be transferred? Should the transfer be made while you are alive or set up in your estate plan? Do you desire to keep some of the income and, if so, how much? If the income is to be kept, should this income be kept so it continues for the benefit of a spouse, sibling, or other person?

Charitable Giving Is Important to You and to Your Community

In 1989, total charitable contributions in the United States were estimated to be $106 *billion*. Sums such as this materially improve our society when they are given to carefully selected groups that will invest the money wisely, monitor its use, and give you assurance that your charitable contribution is meeting a need you feel is important.

In this chapter, you will learn about:

- defined contribution plan
- defined benefit plan
- individual retirement accounts (IRAs)
- Roth IRAs
- limitations on contributions and benefits
- survivor benefits
- borrowing from the plan
- required distributions
- early withdrawals
- distribution alternatives: lump sum/installments/rollovers
- five-year averaging
- tax-free rollovers
- spousal rollovers
- excise taxes
- excess distributions
- estate tax on pensions

15

PENSION PLANS AND IRAS

Pension plans have become an increasingly important source of retirement income for the American public—and an increasingly regulated area of tax law. The resulting complexity means that most people don't understand the intricacies of deferred compensation law.

Today, many people have pension plans. They may have a defined contribution plan, defined benefit plan, 401K, S.E.P., Keough plan, IRA, Roth IRA, or another type of plan, setting aside funds for retirement. These types of retirement plans receive certain tax advantages; typically, money contributed to the plan is not subject to income tax until it is distributed from the plan. Deferral of income tax until the money is received (tax-deferred income) should not be confused with the exemption from tax that is given to certain income, such as interest on some government bonds (tax-exempt or tax-free income).

The Roth IRA differs from the regular IRA in that the regular or older form of IRA defers income tax until the money is withdrawn from the account. However, money contributed to a Roth IRA has already been subject to income taxes so the contributions, together with earnings from the invested money, may be withdrawn tax free. This is a considerable benefit because the earnings on the invested money are never subject to income tax.

It is surprising to see how much money can accumulate in your pension plan. Frequently, you forget this employee benefit until you receive notice from your employer telling you how much has accumulated or has been contributed to the plan. Then you see that your share is larger than you expected. Individual Retirement Accounts (IRAs) also tend to grow rapidly. Since pension plans ordinarily pay no income tax currently, the income they earn is accumulating, and that income is earning income. This compounding of income produces a significant amount of money over an extended period of time.

Pension plans play an important role in estate planning because they are inherently a savings plan for the future, and they frequently have substantial amounts of money. We will look at some of the general rules and approaches to handling pension plans in the estate planning context. While there are many different types of employee benefit plans, generally these plans can be broken down into two broad categories: the defined *contribution* plan and the defined *benefit* plan.

Defined Contribution Plan

The defined contribution plan is based on a fixed contribution. Contributions are made by you as the employee, by your employer, or by both of you, depending on the specific plan your employer uses. The contribution—together with earnings, forfeitures, and other accumulations—gives you a retirement benefit. The amount (or the formula calculating the amount) that the employer contributes each year is fixed and, because of this, the plan is known as a defined or fixed contribution type of plan. On your retirement, you receive the amount that is your share, either as a lump sum or spread out over a period of time for you and a spouse.

Defined Benefit Plan

The other type of plan is the defined benefit plan. Here, the amount the employer contributes is not fixed or defined each year. Rather, the approach is from the other end—that is, the amount you will receive on retirement. Based on this defined amount, each year your employer determines the amount of that year's contribution to your plan. Since the employer's contribution is usually calculated as a percentage of the final average pay, the contribution varies considerably. Each year the contribution is determined by actuarial methods. The employer's contribution depends upon your age, the number of years you have worked for the company, and the number of years it is anticipated that you will remain with the company.

Individual Retirement Accounts

An Individual Retirement Account, or IRA, is one of the most common types of retirement plans. Usually it is an account with a financial institution which is set aside for retirement years. Anyone who works for a salary can have an IRA. However, if you are already a participant in a qualified retirement plan or self-employment plan, or if your adjusted gross income exceeds $25,000 on a single return or $40,000 on a joint return, then the $2,000 contribution to the IRA is no longer tax-free. The contribution to the IRA can still be made, but it is made with after-tax dollars. However, the earnings in the IRA are tax-deferred. If you are not a member of a qualified retirement plan, self-employment plan, or similar plan, you can contribute up to 100% of your earnings or $2,000, whichever is smaller. It is perfectly permissible to have more than one IRA. In fact, in many instances, it is desirable to have more than one IRA. If you have an IRA to which nondeductible contributions were made, this IRA should be kept separate from your deductible contributions. Otherwise the bookkeeping becomes a real headache.

Limitations on Contributions and Benefits

There are limitations on how much can be set aside in pension plans. The Internal Revenue Code says that the employer's contribution for a defined contribution plan must be the lesser of 25% of your compensation or $30,000. The limitation on defined benefit plans is on the maximum that you can receive after retirement. This is approximately the lesser of an indexed dollar amount or 100% of your average compensation (not to exceed $160,000) over your three highest-paid years. The indexed dollar amount is based on cost-of-living adjustments and goes up with the cost of living. For 1998, the indexed dollar amount was $130,000. Notwithstanding the limitation, the plan may provide a minimum annual benefit of $10,000.

Survivor Benefits

Most employer-sponsored pension plans must give the surviving spouse automatic benefits. Generally, this is done in a "qualified joint survivor annuity." This means that the pension plan must be set up in such a way that retirement benefits are paid to the employee; if that employee is deceased, then retirement pension benefits continue to be paid to the surviving spouse. While federal law mandates this requirement, it is subject to a number of exceptions and qualifications. The surviving spouse may waive his or her right to receive the benefits. However, the waiver by a surviving spouse of pension plan benefits must be done perfectly before it will be accepted. For single people, naming someone does not constitute a gift since the designation can always be changed. If, however, a beneficiary who is not a spouse were irrevocably designated to be the beneficiary, this would constitute a gift and gift tax would be applicable. Incidentally, this would be considered to be a gift of a future interest. The $10,000 annual exclusion for gifts would not apply so the first dollar would be charged gift tax.

Borrowing from the Plan

You may want to use the money in the plan without incurring the income tax obligation of a distribution. The government permits loans from a plan under certain circumstances. If the applicable requirements are not met, the loan is considered a distribution and income tax applies. The government will insist that the loan not exceed $50,000 or one-half of the current value of your plan. Plan loans must be repaid under most circumstances within five years. Interest payments must be at a reasonable rate of interest.

Required Distributions

While usual distributions may start as early as age 59½, distributions may be deferred until age 70½. However, the tax law requires that distributions *must* begin when you reach the age of 70½. Failure to take the required amount of money out at this age and thereafter will cause significant tax penalties to arise.

Younger Employees

For a young adult, it may be a good idea to couple the retirement plan with life insurance. Life insurance is a good supplement because pension benefits generally may not begin to be distributed until age 59½. A young person who wants to provide some financial benefit to a spouse or children in the event of his or her death should not count on a retirement plan. Remember, retirement plans typically won't be distributed out until age 59½, and that may be a long time after the death of the young working spouse. Life insurance (Group term life insurance is usually best because of its low premium.) would provide immediate cash at a time when it is needed most. Later, the surviving spouse could draw upon the pension plan after turning 59½.

Early Withdrawals

Sometimes people may want to take their money out of a pension plan before reaching 59½. This is called early withdrawal. The exception to the requirement of being 59½ is if a person is no longer employed by that employer (separated from service); under this exception, distribution may be made at age 55. Also, the government permits early distributions for certain "emergency" needs, such as medical expenses or payments to a divorcing spouse pursuant to a court order issued in connection with the divorce.

There is no similar provision excusing early distributions for emergencies from IRAs.

Early withdrawals from a pension plan or an IRA are subject to a 10% penalty tax to discourage people from taking out the money before retirement. The regular income tax is also applied to these distributions. As a result of this "double tax," the government can take a significant portion of early withdrawals.

Lump Sums, Installments, or Rollovers

Deciding how to take the money out of your pension plan can be difficult. There are three approaches. One is to take it out in a lump sum, pay the tax burden, and have the money. Another alternative is to have the pension money paid out in installments over the anticipated lifetime of you and your spouse. This defers the income tax obligation and lets the pension plan continue to grow; the disadvantage is that you don't have the money. The third alternative is to take the money out of the employer's plan and "roll it over" into an IRA, which you manage yourself.

Five-Year Averaging

The Internal Revenue Code permits certain advantages when you select a lump sum distribution. Recognizing that hardship may result when a lump sum of income pushes you into a higher bracket and is taxed in a single year, the Internal Revenue Code provides that a person can take the pension money and divide it by five. The tax is figured on this one-fifth of the amount of the pension and then that tax is multiplied by five. While dividing by five and then multiplying by five sounds like it would produce the same result, it doesn't. The tax rates are progressive. It is better to have one-fifth of the property taxed at a low rate and then have that multiplied by five rather than have all the property taxed at the top rate.

Tax-Free Rollovers

Sometimes, it is a good idea to take the money out of your employer's pension plan when you retire and put it into a pension plan that you manage yourself. This movement of funds is called a tax-free rollover. An example would be a person who is retiring from a company, wants to take the money, and doesn't want to start paying income tax on it right away. He or she takes the pension plan money and puts it into an IRA. As long as this is done within 60 days from the date of receiving the money, it will be considered a rollover from one plan to another. It is not considered a taxable distribution to the retiring employee. The IRA can be managed by the employee or a money manager and at the same time be tax deferred. A question that occasionally comes up is "Is it necessary to put all the pension money into the IRA?" The answer is no. However, the balance that is kept is not eligible for the five-year averaging mentioned in the preceding paragraph, nor is it free from tax. The amount that you keep will be taxed currently, and the amount that is in the IRA will be tax-deferred.

The Roth IRA

In the beginning of this chapter, we mentioned that the Roth IRA is quite different from a regular IRA. Contributions to the Roth IRA are money which has already been subject to income tax, although distributions from a Roth IRA are withdrawn tax-free. This gives the Roth IRA a number of advantages and makes it a useful estate planning tool. Annual contributions to a Roth IRA are subject to the maximum $2,000 annual contribution. This, of course, means that you may only contribute $2,000 per year. An IRA converted to a Roth IRA is treated as a taxable distribution of the regular IRA. This can produce a considerable income tax and a shock to the taxpayer.

Is it a good idea to roll over the regular IRA into a Roth IRA? The answer to this question depends on the income tax level, the person's life expectancy, anticipated investment outcomes, and a number of other variables. However, as a rule of thumb, it is the author's opinion that if a person anticipates that he or she will live 6 or 7 years after the regular IRA is converted to a Roth IRA, this conversion will produce more money than if the assets were left in the regular IRA and taxes were paid when the money was withdrawn. At first, it seems counterintuitive to pay taxes early, yet remember the tax level maximum would be 40%. This means that it is always true that less than half the money would be consumed by taxes. This also means that the taxpayer gets to keep the lion's share in the Roth IRA since the amount of money that is invested by the taxpayer is more than the amount of money that the government is getting. The taxpayer will come out ahead in the end. With a regular IRA, the government gets to tax all the money, including all the appreciation that occurs in the IRA. With the Roth IRA, the government only gets to tax the amount of money that is put into the Roth IRA and does not get a chance to tax the appreciation. Accordingly, with a Roth IRA, you want to have an opportunity to let the money in the Roth IRA appreciate for a while to pick up this considerable advantage.

There is another advantage to the Roth IRA that should not be over-looked. With a regular IRA, the required distribution dates commence at age 70½. With the Roth IRA, there is no required beginning distribution during the lifetime of the person who creates the Roth IRA. Accordingly, for clients who have been able to accumulate considerable assets, it is pos-sible to defer the required distribution until the death of the owner. In fact, with the Roth IRA, the distribution period can be based on the age of the beneficiary of the Roth IRA following the death of the IRA owner. This suggests another planning opportunity for those persons who have acquired a considerable amount of assets and wish to benefit their grandchildren. Naming a grandchild as beneficiary would provide an opportunity for a long deferral period of the distributions under the Roth IRA, and, as we noted earlier, the longer the distribution period, the more money that can be invested on a tax-free basis and ultimately distributed to the grandchild on a tax-free basis. In this way, the Roth IRA presents a very advantageous estate planning opportunity.

There are some rules to be followed when considering a rollover or a conversion to a Roth IRA. If there is a qualified pension plan, then the con-version must be first from a qualified plan into a regular IRA and then from the regular IRA into a Roth IRA. A rule that causes some taxpayers trou-ble is that a taxpayer cannot make a qualified rollover distribution to a Roth IRA if his or her income exceeds $100,000.

A conversion from a pension plan to a regular IRA to a Roth IRA may be made at any age, but distributions from a pension plan prior to age 59½ may be subject to penalty taxes under the provisions of the plan. If you meet the qualifications for a Roth IRA, then by all means consider setting one up. Roth IRAs are likely to increase in value to the taxpayer as time goes on. The money distributed from a Roth IRA will not be subject to taxes when distributed. Further, funds may be distributed over a long period of time based upon the life expectancy of the beneficiaries, not only the life expectancy of the taxpayer.

Spousal Rollovers

In some cases when a person with an IRA or a pension plan dies and the money goes to the surviving spouse, the surviving spouse does not want the money. What should you do if the money is coming to you and you have to pay taxes on it, but you don't want it yet? Here's the solution: Take the money and "roll it over" into a spousal IRA rollover. Now you're being treated very much as your spouse was. The money can be put into a spousal rollover IRA with no current income tax due. However, you can't take your spouse's IRA and roll it into your pension plan.

Excess Distributions

Prior to its repeal in 1997, there was a special 15% tax on "excessive distributions" from a retirement plan. This tax is no longer applied to distributions.

Estate Tax

Since the pension plan or IRA is an asset the owner earned, this will be included in the owner's estate for estate tax purposes. The beneficiary is usually the spouse, since the federal law now requires that the spouse be the beneficiary unless the spouse waives that right. Since these assets are passing to the surviving spouse and since all assets will pass to the surviving spouse free of estate tax, the IRA or pension plan should not cause any estate tax to arise. In instances where there is no surviving spouse, the usual estate tax rules apply and the IRA or qualified plan may cause substantial estate taxes to arise.

Recalculation

Since regular IRAs are subject to the rule that there are required beginning distribution dates when the participant turns 70½, and that these distributions then follow the taxpayer's life expectancy, the question comes up as to how the life expectancy is to be measured. There are two ways life expectancy can be measured under the IRA distribution rules. One way is to measure the person's life expectancy as of the date of the first distribution. This locks in the distribution schedule. The other way is to recalculate the taxpayer's life expectancy each year. As the person ages, the recalculation will give a longer payout period. However, this cuts both ways. In those instances where the person dies earlier than the anticipated life expectancy, recalculation will catch the deceased taxpayer's estate. Obviously, the life expectancy of a person who was recalculating each year and is now deceased will be zero. Distributions from the IRA are all immediately due. For this reason, many people elect not to recalculate.

Most IRAs provide for recalculation. Accordingly, it may be worthwhile to check if your IRA mandates recalculation. If recalculation is the norm, consider requesting that your personal IRA agreement be changed to take out the automatic recalculation provisions.

IRAs and Pension Plans

As we have seen, the rules concerning IRAs and pension plans are complex. They require careful study because there are so many exceptions to the general statements. The correct answer depends in many instances on when the IRA or pension plan was started, whether the contributions to the IRA were deductible or nondeductible, whether they are the result of a spouse's efforts or your own efforts, whether you are a highly compensated "owner/employee," and many other variables

With careful planning and an awareness of the complexities inherent in such plans, the substantial amounts contained in IRAs and pension plans can be directed to the surviving spouse or dealt with in such a way that planning for retirement and passing assets on to loved ones can be done with a minimum of tax.

In this chapter, you will learn about:

- the benefits of life insurance
- types of available policies
- insurance terms
- interpolated terminal reserve
- assignment of insurance policies
- cash value
- income tax advantages of life insurance
- dividends
- borrowing
- estate tax aspects
- transferring policy ownership
- irrevocable life insurance trust
- how to choose a policy beneficiary
- estate tax treatment
- how to determine the right amount of insurance

16
LIFE INSURANCE

Life insurance is no longer the simple life insurance of past years. New types of policies serve a variety of purposes. Let's look at life insurance in today's world.

In 1941, the Supreme Court described life insurance as "a device to shift and distribute the risk of loss from premature death." Even today, "risk shifting" remains the basic test of whether an arrangement will be considered life insurance and, therefore, entitled to favorable tax treatment. There are statistics ("mortality tables") concerning the life expectancy of an individual of any specific age, the percentage of individuals of the same age who can be expected to die during the year, and any other classification that may be of interest. Insurance companies use these mortality tables to predict the amount of benefits they will have to pay to policy holders. The premiums for traditional life insurance policies are based on the amount of such benefits together with an insurance company's charges, which cover the insurance company's other anticipated costs and expenses and investment results. The new types of policies may contain a separate investment component in addition to insurance protection that accrues to the insured. These investments are funded through higher premiums, the amount of which may fluctuate, often at the policy owner's discretion. Some policies do not even guarantee a minimum death benefit and, therefore, have a substantial built-in element of risk. Because of the proliferation of products intended to serve as tax shelters or short-term investments, Congress enacted new definitions and new rules to identify and govern life insurance for tax purposes.

Traditionally, life insurance was purchased to provide funds for the family after the breadwinner's (then ordinarily the husband's) death. Rarely was there any thought of insuring the wife who worked in the home. Insurance was not intended to be an investment. It was not purchased as a tax-advantaged savings plan. All that has changed in recent years. We'll discuss some of the common types of policies currently available and their advantages and disadvantages, and we'll talk about the economy of purchasing life insurance. Today, some people are more interested in the investment possibilities of life insurance than in the death benefits.

For estate planning, life insurance is still used to replace the earning power of the family breadwinner or, as is more common today, breadwinners. Couples should not overlook the economic value of the services performed by a spouse. Life insurance may be a welcome source of funds after the death of a spouse.

Life insurance is also purchased to provide readily available cash in an estate. Estate taxes become due nine months after the date of death. If cash is not otherwise available, the personal representative of a taxable estate may be forced to sell estate assets at bargain prices to pay taxes. When estate taxes are extremely high, insurance may be the best way to pay these estate taxes.

Another reason to purchase life insurance—a very real reason that is rarely discussed by the life insurance industry or by estate planners—is that after the death of a spouse, there is a feeling of considerable loss. If the survivor is a wife who does not work outside the home or was not included in the management of the family finances, she may have distressing feelings of economic vulnerability. A grieving survivor who has limited experience in managing money and is unfamiliar with the family's financial situation naturally feels a little frightened and very ill at ease when faced with numerous financial decisions and responsibilities after the death of a spouse. Life insurance provides a substantial amount of cash on short notice with few questions or choices. It's comforting to see a large check come from the insurance company and to think "At least I have this." Even when the insurance proceeds are not a financial necessity, they often fill a very real, personal need. The vulnerability and lack of financial acumen of a grieving spouse may be compelling reasons to establish a trust to receive insurance proceeds.

Finally, life insurance can be helpful when a large asset of the estate is ownership in a closely held business (a business owned by a small number of individuals, a family, or other small group). An immediate infusion of cash may be necessary for a variety of reasons—to offset the economic loss the business faces on the death of a person who is important to its operation, to provide the business or remaining owners with sufficient funds to purchase the decedent's share, or to enable the decedent to leave the business to the children who are active in its operation and to give the other children a comparable cash inheritance. This is a complex area that we will cover later in this chapter.

We have seen that life insurance is one way to meet certain real needs of the estate. The cash proceeds, which may be substantial, are available to provide for the emotional well being and comfort of the survivors, to replace the earning power of the breadwinner, to provide liquidity for estate taxes, and to serve possible business purposes. Though not everyone needs or wants life insurance, it should be considered in the estate planning process.

With that brief introduction, let's talk about some of the types of life insurance policies and some of the terms used in the life insurance industry. There are numerous variations of these products, as well as a multitude of available options.

Life Insurance and Estate Taxes

Life insurance in the eyes of the Internal Revenue Service is inherently testamentary. This means that the IRS will seek diligently to apply estate tax to life insurance. All the usual rules about including in an estate the property at its fair market value as of the date of death apply. But in the case of life insurance, the estate also includes any life insurance owned by the decedent or life insurance given away within three years of his or her death. Therefore, life insurance is even more taxable than ordinary property. If Ric gives away $50,000 worth of stocks and bonds and dies within three years, the fair market value of those stocks and bonds at the time of his death is not brought back into his estate. However, if two years before his death, Ric gives away his life insurance policy worth $500,000 on his death—which has a fair market value at the time of his gift of $50,000— the value of this policy is not $50,000. The taxable amount is $500,000, the value as of the date of his death. Life insurance in the estate planning area certainly needs special attention.

Whole Life Insurance

One of the traditional forms of life insurance is called whole life or straight life. Whole life insurance has three components. One is the pure underwriting risk portion of the premium—the mortality risk. This portion is used by the insurance company (the "insurer") solely to offset the expense of paying out the face value of the policy.

The second component is the administrative cost of the policy. After all, the insurance company has to pay for its physical building. It also has to pay its shareholders, officers, employees, and salesmen.

The third component of whole life insurance is the investment factor. Whole life premiums remain level during the life of the policy even though the underwriting risk increases as the insured grows older. During the early years of the policy when the insured is younger, the amount of the premium is higher than the pure actuarial risk of the insured's death. As the policy and the insured become older, the premiums are less than the cost of protection. The excess advance premiums paid in the beginning years are invested by the insurance company. These advance payments result in a cash value within the policy. Most insurance companies allow whole life policy owners to borrow back the paid-in dollars at a reduced interest rate. While the lower rate may justify borrowing from your policy rather than from another source, this feature should be kept in perspective when making the decision to purchase insurance. After all, the company is lending you money which you paid to it in advance and which it is holding for you. Whole life may be preferred by young families getting started because of the savings aspect and because premiums can be paid in installments over the life of the policy.

Endowment Insurance

Endowment insurance functions like whole life but with a set value or face value to be paid out at the end of a particular term. Endowment insurance is not as frequently used in today's insurance marketplace and in fact may gradually be disappearing except in specialized applications.

Universal Life Insurance

Universal life insurance is a relatively recent product. Instead of the traditional savings-type plan of whole life insurance, the universal life policy has a special investment component and, in some instances, risk built in. The universal life policy does not have the level premium that the whole life policy does. Instead, the policy holder may put as much money into the insurance plan as he or she wishes each year. The important thing to remember about universal life insurance is that the owner of the policy, not the insurance company, has the investment control of the life insurance policy. With regular whole life, the insurance company manages the investment factor. With universal, the individual can select from a broad spectrum of investment vehicles ranging from treasury bills to much more aggressive investments. If the owner is wise and lucky in investments, then the value will grow much faster than if regular whole life had been purchased and the insurance company were managing the investments. Conversely, if you do not do as well as the insurance company could, then the value of your policy will be less.

The interest earned by the universal life policy is tax-advantaged. No current tax is paid on the increasing value which results from the investments. Tax is not paid (it is "deferred") until money is actually taken out of the universal life policy. This tax-deferment feature gives the life insurance policy a significant advantage over other types of investments. The money that would have gone to pay income taxes remains with the policy and is available to earn interest. Over a long period of time, the additional value generated by money that would have been paid for taxes can be substantial. For this reason, universal life policies become very popular during periods of high inflation when interest rates and taxes are very high.

Responding to perceived abuses, in 1984 Congress passed strong rules prohibiting certain highly investment-oriented life insurance contracts from being called life insurance and from being treated as life insurance for tax purposes. These 1984 rules require that life insurance policies act more like insurance and less like investment vehicles.

Term Life Insurance

A term life insurance policy is issued by the insurance company for a specific limited period of time, generally one, five, or ten years. The term policy has a lower premium than other types of life insurance because it has no cash value. Premium dollars pay only for the administrative cost and insurance risk that the insured will die before the term of the policy is up. Usually, the premium is established on a yearly basis and increases each year as the insured grows older. If the insured dies during the period of the policy, the designated beneficiary will receive the face amount of the policy. If the policy term ends before the insured's death, the beneficiary receives nothing. There is no value to the policy after the term has passed.

A term policy is also a popular form of insurance for young adults because it provides maximum insurance for the least cash. Some term policies are automatically renewable for a number of years, though premiums usually increase as the insured ages. Another option allows the term policy to be converted into other types of insurance when the higher insurance premiums will not strain the family budget. But term insurance isn't just for young people with limited resources. Sometimes insurance protection is only needed for a specific period of time.

Parents or grandparents may purchase term insurance on the life of one or both parents—renewable for 20 years—at the birth of each child. If a parent dies before the child is 20, this relatively inexpensive policy insures that money will be available to replace the economic support which would have been provided by the parent. The insurance can be a decreasing term policy in which the amount of coverage is reduced as the child grows older, offsetting the increased cost of the insurance. Those concerned about inflation or the cost of college may prefer to keep a level amount of coverage and pay the higher premium each year.

Term policies are frequently used in business transactions when it is desirable to have a party insured for a limited number of years and not for an entire lifetime. One example is a particularly important employee (a "key employee") who is expected to be with the company for ten years. If he or she dies during that period, the company will suffer significant economic loss. For this reason, the company with limited cash to spend on life insurance takes out a term life insurance policy ("key employee insurance") on its employee. The insurance proceeds that will be paid to the company if the insured dies cover at least a portion of the economic loss the company sustains as the result of the death.

Both term and whole life insurance are frequently used in closely held corporations when the corporation and the shareholders agree in advance about the purchase and sale of corporate stock from a decedent stockholder's estate. These contracts ("buy-sell agreements" or "cross-purchase agreements") may require the transfer of shares, allow the corporation a right of first refusal if the shares are to be sold, give the corporation and remaining shareholders the right to purchase the shares, permit the estate to require that the shares be purchased, or whatever else everyone agrees to. Buy-sell agreements and cross-purchase agreements are widely used, with good reason. Rick and Rob may have worked together over the years to build a successful business. When Rick dies, his wife Pat may not want the stock. She needs cash and doesn't care about the business now that Rick is no longer a part of it. Pat typically will have a hard time finding a buyer for Rick's part interest in the corporation. Rob has a valid concern—but no control—over who buys the shares. With the insurance proceeds, Rob can buy Rick's shares of stock and Pat will get the value of her husband's shares.

When there is a buy-sell agreement requiring the purchase of stock, and it is funded with life insurance, each shareholder can be assured of a cash purchaser for his or her closely held corporate stock. With the insurance in place, the surviving shareholders know the necessary cash will be available to pay for the deceased shareholder's stock. All this can be accomplished for a relatively low premium.

Single Premium Life Insurance

Sometimes it makes good economic sense to pay all the life insurance premiums of a policy at one time, so there is a single premium life insurance. This type of policy has aspects of whole life, but instead of relatively small premiums being paid out over a long period of time, the premiums are all grouped together, a credit is given for early payment, and the single premium is paid. The life insurance is then in force for the lifetime of the individual. Single premium policies are frequently used by people who are in high-income tax brackets and have enough cash to make a substantial payment. By making this early payment, they receive the income tax benefit of tax deferral. Having the insurance company invest the advance payment portion of their premium is like having a savings account which earns interest tax-deferred until withdrawal. There are policies that allow the insured to decide whether the funds are invested in stocks, bonds, real estate, or other forms of investment. Of course, the more control the individual has over the investment, the less the policy looks like insurance.

In estate planning, single premium policies are also used as gifts. A wealthy individual can purchase a substantial single premium life insurance policy on her or his own life and transfer it to a trust or an individual or a charity. The single premium which has been paid in a lump sum will be considerably less than the face value of the policy. When the policy is transferred by gift, the value for gift tax purposes is very close to the cash value of the policy. Assuming that a relatively young person could purchase a $100,000 face value policy for a lump sum premium cost of $30,000 or less, the policy could be given to three individuals without any transfer tax. (Remember, the insured can transfer $10,000 or more per year per beneficiary free of gift tax.) With three individuals owning the policy, that's the $30,000 actual cash value of the policy, even though it has a face value on the insured's death of $100,000. If the insured dies, $100,000 of value has been transferred out of his or her estate at no actual transfer tax cost. However, as we will see later in this chapter, there are some significant problems in transferring life insurance that is owned by the insured. It is much better for the insured to transfer the cash to the individuals who will ultimately own the policy and have the premiums paid by them than to purchase the policy and transfer it.

Second-to-Die Life Insurance

One of the more recent items being offered by the life insurance industry is known as joint life insurance, survivorship coverage, or "second-to-die" coverage. The thrust of this type of life insurance is that the coverage insures more than one life. The death benefit is payable only upon the death of the second insured. Typically, these policies are on the lives of a husband and wife.

As we saw earlier, in most situations involving a husband and wife in a long-term marriage, there will be no tax upon the death of the first spouse because of the complete marital deduction for assets passing to the surviving spouse. The life insurance industry created the second-to-die coverage to provide liquidity to estates at the time the second spouse dies, when substantial amounts of cash are needed to pay estate taxes.

Premiums are remarkably low for second-to-die coverage. The reason for this is that insuring two people increases the life expectancy actuarially. The cost of the mortality risk is less than insuring just the younger person alone. After all, there is always the outside chance, which actuaries and other persons who study mortality tables must consider, that the younger person will be killed in an accident or unexpectedly develop a fatal illness. In fact, sometimes it can be very useful to use second-to-die coverage when one of the parties is essentially uninsurable because of health problems or advanced age. The insurance company will accept the mortality risk of insuring the unhealthy or older person when coupled with the healthy or younger person, and the premiums are not excessive. Second-to-die life insurance is also used in estate planning as part of a gifting program to provide funds to pay estate taxes. Frequently with this type of insurance, the funds to purchase are transferred by the parents to the children. The children then use these funds to purchase the policy. The children name themselves as the owners of the policy and as the beneficiaries of the policy proceeds. The insureds are the parents of the children. The policy does not pay when one parent dies, only when the surviving parent dies. Since the children are the beneficiaries of the insurance policy, they now have substantial amounts of money with which to pay the estate taxes or to use as an inheritance.

Terminology

After this short overview of the types of policies, let's look at a few of the more commonly used terms in life insurance. Many people may be unaware that the designations of owner, insured, and beneficiary in their life insurance policies have very significant consequences. The owner of the policy is the individual who has the right to change the policy, cash it in, modify it, or give it to some other person. The insured is the person whose life is being covered by the insurance policy. The beneficiaries are those who would receive the money from the insurance company upon the insured's death. The insurance company, by contract with the owner, has agreed to pay the value of the policy to the beneficiary if the insured dies.

These concepts are pretty simple. The problem arises in failing to think through who the owner should be, who the insured should be, and who the beneficiaries should be. All too frequently, the insured is the owner. If the insured is the owner at the time of death, the full face value of the insurance policy will be included in his or her estate. For this reason, it is often better for estate planning purposes to have someone other than the insured own the policy.

Interpolated Terminal Reserve Value

The interpolated terminal reserve value is the value that the IRS uses when calculating the value of most life insurance policies for gift tax purposes. Generally, the cash value and the interpolated terminal reserve value are similar except in the first few years, when the interpolated terminal reserve is generally significantly lower.

It is important to establish the value of a life insurance policy before making a gift of the policy. Most insurance companies will provide you with interpolated terminal reserve value. If your insurance agent is not familiar with this term, you need to be firm and insist that the agent ask the company for the amount. Gift splitting between spouses in connection with the annual exclusion from gift tax can be used to make gifts of insurance. If the owner of the policy is married and the spouse joins in the gift, the couple can give away a life insurance policy with a current value of $20,000 or more without incurring any gift tax, provided this is the only gift they make to that individual during the calendar year. They must, of course, file an informational joint gift tax return, but no tax is due. Also, the marital deduction for gift tax applies to the transfer of a life insurance policy to a spouse. An unlimited amount of life insurance may be given to a spouse as a gift without any gift tax.

Cash Value

The cash value of a policy is the amount of money you can get if you "cash in" your policy with the insurance company. Whole life policies frequently have a substantial cash value because of the savings component in the premiums. On the other hand, term insurance has no cash value because the premiums are solely the actuarial risk that the insured may die before the actuarial tables say he or she will. Usually, term payments are on a year-to-year basis. In any event, the cash value is almost always significantly less than the face value that is due when the insured dies. For example, Ric owns a $100,000 term policy issued on a year-to-year basis on the life of his wife, Gina. If Gina dies during the term of the policy, their children (the beneficiaries) receive the $100,000 face value of the policy. On the other hand, if Ric dies during the term of the policy and Gina is still alive, the value of this term insurance, which is an asset of Ric's estate, might be less than $500.

Because of the difference between cash value and face value, people frequently make gifts of life insurance. They know that the transfer tax cost is based on the cash value or interpolated terminal reserve, whichever is higher, but the value for estate tax purposes (if the policy is still owned by the insured) is the death proceeds, which are always higher—usually much higher.

Assignment of Insurance Policies

Assignment of insurance policies is quite common. Banks frequently ask to have any insurance policies assigned to them insuring the life of a debtor. This way, the banks are more certain that they are going to be paid if the debtor dies. The beneficiary is the person who receives the death benefit proceeds. If there is a loan outstanding on these death benefit proceeds, the amount that the individual beneficiary actually gets is reduced by this loan value.

Dividends

Some insurance companies pay dividends on their insurance. This sounds like a dividend on stock, but it is different. The dividend on a life insurance policy is a return of excess premium. Sometimes an insurance company will find that it has excess premiums because of unforeseen but favorable circumstances. It will do one of three things: send back some of these excess premiums in the form of a cash dividend, provide an additional year's coverage for "free," or allow the dividend to be used as payment for additional amounts of insurance.

Borrowing

Borrowing against insurance policies frequently makes good sense. Under the older types of policies, the rate of interest charged for borrowing against the policy is very low compared to contemporary interest rates. Because of this, people sometimes will borrow against their life insurance policies to receive the loan proceeds and then buy more life insurance with the proceeds. That borrowed money is "cheaper" than if they had taken the money from somewhere else because the "cost" of the money is less when borrowing against the policy than from other sources. However, these loans, usually at favorable interest rates, cause interest to be assessed, and these interest expenses on life insurance policies are treated like any other form of consumer interest: They are not deductible under the tax law. So, in reality, the old adage about borrowing against your life insurance policy and investing the proceeds as being sound financial management no longer applies as often because of the change in the tax law. The loss of the interest deduction, the decline in interest rates, and the fact that the interest is fully taxable cause the financial planner to calculate carefully before recommending that someone borrow against his or her life insurance policy.

Life Insurance and Income Taxes

Since we're looking at life insurance as an investment vehicle as well as a way of providing easily accessible cash, let's look at how life insurance is treated for income tax purposes. Life insurance does have some tax advantages. While it is probably not correct to say that life insurance is income tax-free, it certainly is correct to say it is income tax-advantaged. If you invest $100 in stock, you must pay capital gains on that stock if it goes up when you sell it. In the meantime, you must pay ordinary income tax on the dividends produced by that stock. Similarly, if you take that same $100 and invest it in a treasury obligation, a CD, or some other interest-yielding investment, you must pay income tax each year on that interest. However, when you give that same money to an insurance company and purchase whole life insurance, you do not have to pay income tax on the investment part of your premium. The "invested" money is free to grow. By being reinvested, it earns more interest, which is reinvested and earns even more interest.

However, like all things, there comes a time when the piper must be paid, particularly if the owner is seeking lifetime benefits. If you take out of the life insurance investment plan more than you put in, you must pay income taxes on the excess over the amount that was paid in. These are considered to be ordinary income payments and are taxed at the ordinary income rate. The government considers that you first get back the money you put in, and what you get back above that amount is treated like interest or dividends.

Upon the insured's death, when the beneficiary receives the death benefits, the lump sum paid to the beneficiary is free from income tax. Sometimes the death benefit proceeds are left with the insurance company under one of the settlement options the insurance companies offer. Under some of the settlement options, the interest earned by those death benefits is free of income tax until distributed.

The 1986 tax law significantly changed the picture concerning the income tax consequences of withdrawing funds from certain types of life insurance policies. Generally, withdrawals may be made from a life insurance policy's cash values without incurring an income tax. However, these withdrawals are usually treated as income in the case of withdrawals within 15 years after a universal life insurance policy is set up. Hence, owners of universal life insurance policies should be extremely cautious about withdrawals. In fact, if any life insurance policy does not meet certain requirements, withdrawing funds from the policy can cause income taxes to arise unexpectedly. Never take withdrawals from a policy until you check the income tax consequences. The next question then becomes, "What type of treatment does the insurance policy receive under the estate tax law?"

Estate Tax Aspects

The estate tax aspects of life insurance are perhaps some of the most interesting areas in the whole field of estate tax. First of all, we're dealing with what are typically large amounts of very liquid assets, which may be subject to very high tax levels. Further, special rules apply to life insurance to make it more taxable than any other type of asset. It is easier to make a mistake on the naming of owners and beneficiaries of life insurance than of other assets.

Frequently, life insurance is included in the estate because the person who died was the owner of the policy. If the decedent had any aspects of ownership at all, then it is likely that this insurance policy will be included in the insured-owner's estate. For this reason, in a taxable estate, it is almost always desirable to have someone other than the insured own the policy. Having the insured and the owner be the same person is a sure way to increase the estate tax and reduce the ultimate amount that will go to the beneficiaries.

If the insurance proceeds are to be paid to the trustee of a living trust or to the personal representative of an estate, these proceeds or death benefits will be included in the owner's estate. The full cash value will be taxed upon death. The estate tax starts at 37% and goes to 55%, so the estate tax on this insurance money can be very high. It is better to have the owner and the beneficiary be a surviving spouse or perhaps another beneficiary if there is no surviving spouse. In this way, the proceeds will not be payable to the personal representative or to the trustee, and will not be included in the estate for this reason.

Transfer of Ownership

For reasons noted above, people frequently gift the ownership of an existing policy. To keep the insurance proceeds out of the insured's estate, the insured must transfer all rights of any type of ownership in the policy. There must be a complete and full transfer with no strings attached. The owner must give up the right to change the beneficiary, to surrender the policy, to pledge it for a loan, or to cash in its cash surrender value. The transfer of the ownership must take place at least three years before the insured dies, and the likelihood of the owner ever getting the policy back must be less than one chance in 20.

If there is a greater chance than one in 20, or if the owner dies within three years after transferring the policy, or if there are any "strings" on the transfer, the IRS will add the value of the policy back into the estate. What this means is that it is very important to transfer all incidents of ownership. Because of these special rules, life insurance, far from being one of the least taxable items in an estate, is one of the most taxable items.

Irrevocable Life Insurance Trust

Irrevocable life insurance trusts have been with us for some time. What are these? What do they do? What good do they do? The irrevocable life insurance trust is, first of all, a trust. A trust is created and an individual or corporation is named to serve as trustee. The beneficiary is always someone other than the person creating the trust, and the trust is irrevocable. This means it is cast in stone. You may be wondering, "Why would you ever want to create a trust which is cast in stone and which you could never change, amend, alter, revoke, or have anything to do with ever again?" The answer lies in the nature of life insurance and the estate tax law.

At the time of purchase, life insurance always costs significantly less than the death benefit. Some clever person might say, "I have an idea! I will purchase some life insurance and put it in an irrevocable trust so it is completely out of my estate. When I die, the face value of that policy will be paid to my beneficiaries, but it will never be taxed. I didn't own it at the time of my death and therefore there could be no estate tax on it." In fact, this clever approach has been used. However, the government felt it was losing too much estate tax revenue. It then passed a law which said you could not transfer life insurance to a trust and then die within three years without having that property taxed to your estate.

Buying life insurance and then gifting it is a disaster on two counts. First, the full face value may be included in your estate and will generate a great deal of estate tax. Second, there's no extra money to pay the estate taxes. While the insurance is included in the estate for tax purposes, the actual money on that policy goes to the beneficiaries. They are not obligated to provide money to pay for the estate tax unless certain uncommon provisions were inserted in the will.

The Prearrangement Problem with Irrevocable Life Insurance Trusts

Therefore, people very soon stopped transferring life insurance into these irrevocable life insurance trusts. They said, "If we don't transfer the life insurance, then maybe what we ought to do is transfer money into the trust. We'll let the trustee buy the life insurance." This works in many, but not all, instances. After all, the government does know what is going on. And most people won't transfer substantial amounts of money to the trust unless they know what the trustee is going to do with that money.

Frequently, people will decide on an amount of life insurance and find out what the premiums will be. Then they set up a trust and transfer that amount of cash or assets into the trust. Not too surprisingly, the trustee decides to purchase life insurance and has just the right amount of money to pay the premiums. The IRS does not like this practice. There have been a number of cases dealing with this and similar types of problems involving irrevocable life insurance trusts. The government has tried many tactics to cause the face value of the policy to be included in the estate, even though the person who died did not own the policy and never had.

The IRS has had some success in attacking prearranged insurance trusts. In a 1989 case out of Miami, the IRS asserted that the trustee of the irrevocable life insurance trust was acting as the "mere agent" of the insured. The insured arranged for the policy, decided on the coverage, went through the medical examination, and transferred funds to the trust sufficient to pay the premiums each year. All in all, the government said this was a "done deal." Everything was set up ahead of time. It remains to be seen what will happen in similar cases in the future. For the time being, Floridians contemplating setting up irrevocable life insurance trusts should be careful not to place their estates in a situation where the government may assert that the face value of the policy is included in their estate for estate tax purposes. This is a very undesirable result.

On the other hand, when the irrevocable life insurance trust works, it works very well. Maybe you're thinking about buying some term insurance. This is the type of insurance that insures you on a year-to-year basis. It has a relatively low premium for a relatively high payoff on death. Rather than just buying it in your own name and having it included in your estate, you set up an irrevocable life insurance trust. The bank down the street agrees to serve as trustee for a reasonable fee. You transfer $4,500 to the trust every year. Each year, the trustee buys term insurance. You create this trust at age 55 as a nonsmoker. Five years later, you die. A reasonable face amount for this term insurance to pay would be $600,000 upon death.

Look what's happened. You have shifted $22,500 out of your estate and yet the beneficiaries of that trust, who may well be your children or grandchildren, get $600,000 tax-free. The money can be used by the trustee for their health, maintenance, support, and education. Funds in the trust can be used to make sure that your grandchildren go to college or that your children have additional funds for retirement—all free of estate taxes. There has been a tremendous savings. This is the reason people keep coming back to irrevocable life insurance trusts. They provide an excellent vehicle for transferring assets free of estate tax. But while the taxpayer sees this as a tremendous opportunity, the IRS still sees it as too good for the taxpayer.

Who Should the Beneficiary of the Policy Be?

Although it's not an absolute rule, naming your estate as beneficiary of your insurance policy is usually not a good choice. This will cause the policy proceeds to be subject to federal estate tax if the total estate exceeds the applicable exemption amount and increases per year.

Suppose the estate is not subject to estate tax because it is not going to exceed the exempt amount. Someone may say it doesn't make any difference then, and it is just as easy to have the policy payable to the estate. Many would not argue with this point. However, that same someone should also mention that, by making the policy proceeds payable to the estate, you increase the size of the probate estate and will probably increase the costs in administering the estate (probate expense). Sometimes this is the only logical way to handle the proceeds because they are to be divided among a number of people. However, if you do not have a number of beneficiaries, it is better to have the policy proceeds paid directly to the beneficiary. The beneficiary will get the money faster and the money he or she receives will not be subject to personal representatives' and attorneys' fees.

How Much Insurance?

How much insurance you should carry is one of the most important questions and sometimes the most difficult. To know the correct answer requires a well-operating crystal ball. However, even without supernatural guidance, it is possible to make some educated guesses as to how much insurance you need. Various rules of thumb exist: eight times your earnings, ten times earnings, or maybe five times earnings. Not surprisingly, many life insurance agents push for the higher multiple in hopes of selling a larger insurance policy. The use of such rules of thumb may work in some areas, but they can be worse than useless for life insurance and may give the insured an unwarranted sense of security. If the decision based on an earning multiple is in fact the right amount, it is solely the result of luck.

Step-by-Step Plan

Let's consider a step-by-step plan for deciding how much life insurance you need for estate purposes. First, figure your current assets and liabilities, and be very honest about them. If you are careful in listing your assets, you will probably be surprised at their total value. Since you are looking at life insurance from an estate tax standpoint, put down the full value of joint property held with a surviving spouse. The full value of these properties will be subject to tax upon the death of the surviving spouse, so the full value is important.

Second, project the values of the assets and liabilities out to a reasonable period, say five to ten years from now. If you figure further out than this, you're merely speculating, and a shorter period of time may not be very helpful either.

Third, see if your estate plan provides for the payment of estate taxes on your death or if these estate taxes will be deferred until the death of the surviving spouse through use of the marital deduction. Be sure you are satisfied with your estate plan and that you have all the necessary documents to successfully carry out that plan.

Fourth, compute the estate taxes that would be due on your estate using the values and liabilities five or ten years out. Be sure to add in any administration costs and other expenses to which your estate may be subjected. If you have a corporate executor, anticipate that the charge will probably be between 2% and 3% of the estate. If your assets are passing through probate, anticipate that the cost of carrying these assets through probate will be approximately 2% to 4% for attorneys' fees. If your assets are passing through an *inter vivos* trust, anticipate that your corporate trustee will charge you 2% to 3% for handling these assets and approximately 1% for attorneys' fees, and that there will be additional charges for preparing estate tax returns, which should be figured in at approximately one-half of 1%.

A word of caution about these numbers: It is impossible to make accurate estimates for every possible situation that could occur in the state of Florida. Some personal representatives will charge more; others less. Family members may charge nothing at all to act as personal representative. Attorneys' fees vary considerably depending on the time, responsibilities, and difficulties involved, among other factors. It is not considered bad form to ask your attorney what he or she estimates the legal fees would be on the estate if the estate were administered today and there were no unusual complications. Your attorney should be able to give you a reasonable range of figures.

After you look at what the anticipated estate taxes will be, see if there is a way to decrease this cost. Would it be better to go to a type of estate plan that defers the estate taxes, or would it be better to pay some taxes initially? Deferring taxes is always appealing. In some instances, however, it is better to pay the estate taxes at the first death. Property that is taxed at the time the first spouse dies can appreciate without having the increased value subject to tax at the death of the surviving spouse. Because the rate of estate tax increases as the value of the estate increases, you can usually get some benefit from the lower rates when both spouses pay some taxes.

These decisions generally require a considerable amount of working with the numbers and assumptions of growth rates, present value of dollars, and other factors. Most people, however, opt to defer the estate tax in its entirety, using the applicable exemption (see Chapter 9) to shelter the first $600,000+ from tax and passing the balance to a surviving spouse. If there are substantial assets, the $600,000+ may be given outright to individuals other than the spouse. More often, a trust (a "credit shelter trust") is used so that the income from the $600,000+ will be available for the surviving spouse during his or her life before being distributed to the other individuals.

It is now time for a word of comfort. If you have been doing some of these computations, you realize that there is a tremendous number of assumptions being made in each step. You don't know how the estate tax law is going to change or even what the estate tax rates will be. You don't know whether you will still have the full marital deduction or a $600,000+ applicable exemption. You don't know what the growth rate of money is going to be or how your assets will change in value. You don't know what your expenses and debts are likely to be. In short, there are many assumptions which necessarily cause this exercise to produce only a best guess. However, it is the best guess that you can make. Having considered these matters, you may want to purchase additional life insurance. If, at the time the taxes are due, it looks as though the estate will have substantial liquidity because of cash, publicly traded securities, or a buy-sell agreement for closely held stock, for example, then the money to pay these taxes may not have to be raised through life insurance. It may be possible simply to sell the securities. They will have a date-of-death basis even if they were bought for much less years ago, so there should be little or no capital gains tax.

On the other hand, your assets may be highly illiquid, or held in forms not readily converted to cash, such as stock in closely held companies and real estate. In this case, it may be desirable to have more life insurance to provide cash to pay the taxes due within nine months of death. Some people purchase life insurance with the hope of leaving a larger estate to their children.

Another factor to consider is the financial needs of your spouse following your death. If your spouse has substantial assets or a job that provides a sufficient income for your family, the need for insurance on your life decreases.

All in all, the question of how much life insurance to have cannot be readily reduced to rules of thumb. The questions and answers in this chapter will lead you to a general sense of how much life insurance you need. At that point, you are better equipped to decide how much life insurance you need than you would have been in trying to apply an arbitrary rule of thumb. Even after making the review and considering all the factors in determining how much life insurance seems appropriate, don't forget that just as your life changes, so does your need for life insurance. Refer to your assumptions every three or five years. Are there changes in family situations or personal financial situations? What about inflation? Is there more discretionary money so that the cost of buying some additional life insurance wouldn't cut into the family budget in such a large way?

Summary

We have discussed most of the different types of life insurance—whole life, term life, universal life, single premium, and second-to-die. You have seen how life insurance is treated for income tax and estate tax purposes. You also have seen a step-by-step plan for determining how much life insurance you need. Life insurance can be confusing for the layman, but it offers liquidity and security at a time when these two items can be very important to those left behind.

In this chapter, you will learn:

- what probate is
- what is necessary to get probate started
- why it takes so long
- who can be a personal representative
- what the duties of personal representatives (executors) are
- how creditors' claims and distributions are handled

17

PROBATE

So much has been said about probate, it seems appropriate to include a short chapter on it in this book on estate planning. Estate planning looks to the probate process and to what happens during administration of a person's estate. You should have a passing familiarity with what happens in probate if you are to have a full understanding of estate planning for the Floridian.

Probate in Florida differs from probate in many states in that the procedure and even the philosophy in Florida reflect a feeling that the process should be free of judicial activism. This feeling is much stronger here than in other states. The greater weight of the responsibility for the administration of a person's estate falls on the attorney and the personal representative (executor). They are the persons responsible for seeing that the deceased person's assets are handled as he or she wished.

Probate involves marshalling assets, paying bills, filing tax returns, and doing the other things that must be done after a person dies. Actually, the word comes from a Latin word meaning "to prove." Its most narrow definition is the action of proving the will as being the final will. In general terms, however, probate is the entire process of handling an estate with the lawyers and courts from the beginning of the court proceeding through the final distribution of assets to the beneficiaries and the closing of the estate.

We will talk about what actually happens on a day-to-day basis in a typical estate. What do the attorneys do? What do the personal representatives do? What do the judges do? What is the point of all this?

Initial Conference with Attorney

Let's look at what might be called a typical estate of a man we will call Adam Nemo. We begin with a call from one of Mr. Nemo's children to the attorney's office telling us that Mr. Nemo has passed away. She has come down to be with her mother, the widow, and wants to know what to do. In many instances, the response will be to take care of family matters and notify friends and relatives who should receive word of Mr. Nemo's death. When it is convenient for the family, Mrs. Nemo and the children should meet with the attorney to discuss the estate. The attorney will probably also tell them that when they come in, they should bring with them a general idea of Mr. Nemo's assets, death certificates as they are usually available, and Mr. Nemo's will.

The family comes in to the attorney's office, bringing the will, a number of papers reflecting financial information, and a host of questions. While it is high drama and beloved by movie producers, the attorney usually does not formally gather the family together and in solemn tones "read the will." Usually, the family has already read the will. They know exactly what it says. The will is written in reasonably clear English, and they have no difficulty understanding what Mr. Nemo had to say and what he wanted to have done with his assets. Their concerns now are "What do we do next? How long will this take and how much will it cost?"

PETITION FOR ADMINISTRATION

Order Admitting a Will to Probate and Appointing a Personal Representative

Commencement of the estate is done with the filing of the Petition for Administration. This probate court form and other typical probate court forms discussed in the following paragraphs are in Appendix L. The Petition states that Mr. Nemo has died, states his residence, and names his next of kin. It requests that Mrs. Nemo, the person named in his will, be appointed as the personal representative and gives the court an idea of the general nature of the assets and whether a federal estate tax return will be filed.

Oath of Personal Representative, Designation of Resident Agent, and Acceptance

The court will require an Oath of Personal Representative and Designation of Resident Agent. The Oath is a solemn assurance that the person seeking to be personal representative will be diligent in administering the estate. The Designation of Resident Agent designates the person—typically the attorney—who will be served with any legal papers if the personal representative is not available.

Letters of Administration

When the Petition and Oath are filed, together with the original will and the court filing fee of approximately $114, the court will review the Petition, Oath, and will. If satisfied that everything seems to be correct, the judge will enter an order directing that the will be admitted as the Last Will and Testament of Mr. Nemo. The court will further direct that Letters of Administration be issued to Mrs. Nemo as the personal representative after she posts a bond. A bonding company agrees to post a bond that Mrs. Nemo will carry out her duties as personal representative; if she does not and instead steals the money, the bonding company will make up the loss. Courts typically will waive the filing of a fiduciary bond if the will directs that no bond be posted and if the person is a resident of Florida. If a person dies without a will, the courts will require a bond in full out of the estate, which significantly increases the cost of administering the estate. Since Mrs. Nemo lives in Florida and the will waives bond, the court will not require a bond, and Letters of Administration are issued to Mrs. Nemo.

Letters of Administration are formal authorizations from the court to any person who has assets or financial information of Mr. Nemo's. Anyone having assets or information concerning Mr. Nemo is directed to give this information to the person appointed as his personal representative—in this case, Mrs. Nemo. This gives the personal representative full authority to find all assets and to request bank accounts or other information necessary to marshal the assets. In many instances, the attorney will ask the personal representative to sign a form directed to any person having information concerning Mr. Nemo's assets asking that he or she release this information to a law firm or attorney. This will save the personal representative a great deal of time. If general inquiries are made, the personal representative, by signing this form, can have the attorney write the various financial institutions and request that they respond in writing, providing information concerning bank accounts, savings accounts, certificates of deposit, outstanding loans, or any other necessary information. Once the Letters of Administration are issued, the estate is now formally opened and the personal representative is in business.

Proof of Service and Notice of Administration

Once the personal representative has been appointed, a Notice of Administration will appear in the newspaper or will be otherwise published. The purpose of the Notice of Administration is two-fold. First, it tells creditors that if they have any claims against the estate, they should file a claim form with the court within three months advising the personal representative of their claim. If the creditors are notified that they should file such a claim and fail to do so, they may be barred for failure to file a claim within three months, as provided in the notice. The United States Supreme Court has ruled that the personal representative has a duty to tell creditors (or people who may be creditors) that the person has died, that creditors should file a claim in court, and that failure to file a claim may cause it to be barred.

The second purpose of the Notice of Administration is to tell people that Mr. Nemo's will has been admitted by the court as his Last Will and Testament and that his estate is being administered. If anyone objects to the will or the person serving as personal representative, the objecting person has three months in which to object formally after receiving this notice. If he or she fails to do so within three months, it will be difficult to later start a will contest or similar action. These notices are typically published in the newspaper so creditors get as much notice as possible.

Inventory and Proof of Service of Inventory

While the Notice of Administration's three-month period is running, the diligent personal representative will compile a list of Mr. Nemo's assets and liabilities, at least to the best extent possible. The list of assets will come from Mr. Nemo's financial papers, as well as from financial institutions with whom he had dealt and other sources such as business associates. Once the information concerning financial assets is available, the Inventory will be filed with the court. The Inventory will list any homestead and any non-homestead real estate, as well as other property, which would include items such as furniture, furnishings, automobiles, bank accounts, stocks, bonds, and other types of assets. It is worth noting here again that while this Inventory is filed with the court, it is not available to anyone who might want to read it just to find out "what he was worth." Only people who have a need to know what the assets are can read the Inventory. Persons with a need to know are beneficiaries or creditors concerned about their unpaid claims who want to assure themselves that there are sufficient assets to pay the claims.

Personal Representative's Proof of Claim

Once the three-month Notice of Administration period has ended, the Inventory will have been filed and the personal representative and attorney will know the approximate value of the assets in the estate and also any claims outstanding in the estate. The next step is to pay off creditors and to distribute the estate to the beneficiaries. In many instances, this process takes five or six months. But it frequently takes longer than this because of factors beyond the control of the attorney or personal representative. If Mr. Nemo's assets exceed the applicable exclusion amount of $600,000+, a federal estate tax return must be filed.

The initial petition requires the personal representative to tell the court whether or not he or she believes that a federal estate tax return will be filed. The reason for this is that the court will check and ask the personal representative to close the estate if a year has passed since the probate estate was started. If there is an estate tax return to be filed, the court knows that it may well be 18 months from the date of death before the personal representative can close the estate because of the time requirements imposed by the federal government while the IRS reviews the federal estate tax return.

Frequently, if there are dollar gifts in the will, these will be taken care of at the end of the three-month period, leaving a substantial reserve to cover contingencies that might arise for the payment of the federal estate taxes. The personal representative may be personally liable for unpaid federal taxes on the federal estate tax return and will want to be sure there are plenty of assets in the estate to cover any tax liabilities. These tax liabilities might also include past unpaid income taxes, withholding taxes or intangible taxes, or inheritance or estate taxes. The personal representative may also sell assets. Sometimes, if the person who has died does not have a surviving spouse, the children will want to sell the real estate in Florida to raise cash and to reduce the expense of maintaining the property. They frequently will discuss this with the attorney and contact a real estate broker in order to get the property on the market early during administration of the estate.

Accountings

Since the personal representative is handling other people's money, he or she has to file accountings. Accountings can be handled in one of two ways: formal court accountings (listing all assets, receipts, and disbursements) and simplified accountings. Many attorneys and beneficiaries prefer simplified accountings which show the inventory values, income coming in, disbursements going out, and remaining balance available for distribution to the beneficiaries. These informal accountings cover all the information that most beneficiaries need to be assured that the estate has in fact been properly handled. Once they receive this information, if they are entirely satisfied with the way the estate has been managed, they may file a consent saying that they have received an accounting, that they are satisfied with the accounting, and that they waive any formal court accounting. This occurs in probably the majority of estates because it is a simple way to handle accountings, and it speeds up the settlement of the estate.

If the beneficiaries are not satisfied, the personal representative will file a formal accounting in court. The beneficiaries will be given copies of the accounting and told to review it and file any objections. The judge reviews the objections and can require the personal representative to respond to concerns that the beneficiaries have as to the administration of the estate, particularly regarding the personal representative's accounting. In our case, Mrs. Nemo was the sole beneficiary. As such, she did not have to file any accounting if she did not wish to.

Final Distribution, Petition for Discharge, and Order of Discharge

Once the beneficiaries are satisfied with the proceedings in the estate, the personal representative will make a distribution of the remaining assets to the beneficiaries. The beneficiaries will file their receipts and waivers as to further proceedings. The beneficiaries sign the waiver stating that they are satisfied with the way the estate has been handled, that they have received their share of the estate, and that they are content that the estate may now be closed. The personal representative, upon receiving these consents and waivers from beneficiaries, files the Petition for Discharge. This shows that the interested parties have all consented to the way the estate has been handled and asks that the personal representative be discharged from any further responsibility in connection with the estate. The judge typically enters these orders after reviewing the file: he or she wants to be satisfied with everything that has taken place.

Summary

As we have described it, the probate process makes sense and sounds fairly simple. Why, then, does it take so long and cost so much? Actually, the probate part of handling an estate shouldn't cost so much. What takes a lot of time and causes some of the expense are all the related matters that come up in handling a person's estate. There are hundreds of questions that come up regarding income taxes, estate taxes, intangible taxes, cash needs, joint property, Medicare, Blue Cross/Blue Shield, how to handle particular assets, what to do about social security, problems with beneficiaries, and all the other complexities with which human life is so richly woven.

CONCLUSION

We've come a long way. We started by discussing estate planning for the Floridian. That estate planning process began with thinking about estate planning not only in the context of dollars and cents, but also in terms of each individual and what's best for him or her. We have covered a great deal of ground, hopefully in a way less painful than is suggested by the complexities involved in estate planning. This is one of the more complex areas of the law. It deals simultaneously with the highly technical aspects of the Internal Revenue Code and also with the very vague and general question of what is best for all concerned.

We worked through the usual documents—wills, powers of attorney, living wills, and living trusts. Then we gradually took on the more complicated areas of homestead, estate and gift taxes, charitable giving, and life insurance, and we moved on even further through charitable remainder trusts, irrevocable life insurance trusts, and some of the less common estate planning documents. To be sure, there are still more exotic aspects: Estate planning is a very fluid and, at times, rapidly changing discipline.

Occasionally, a new concept and document may appear on the scene but is rarely the magic bullet everyone is looking for. It is unlikely that such a magic bullet will ever be invented. Although it pays to stop and carefully analyze anything new on the estate planning horizon, most things turn out to be not quite as good as originally described. However, there may be strong reasons for using them. Living trusts are a good example—neither a quack remedy nor a miracle cure.

When considering estate planning, it is always a good idea to consult a qualified professional. Too much money is riding on the outcome to try to do things inexpensively or single-handedly. Always seek help from a qualified estate planning attorney: Such help is one of the best bargains going. He or she can show you how to save you and your beneficiaries money and, at the same time, set the stage so that your assets can be managed and transferred to your beneficiaries in a way that reflects your personal goals and philosophy.

It is my hope that, with the tools described in this book, Floridians will be equipped with a clear understanding of the basic concepts of estate planning and will be able to apply these concepts to their own lives. Their wealth will transmitted from one generation to another responsibly, quickly, and inexpensively.

APPENDICES

APPENDIX A
ASSET SCHEDULE

Include the approximate value of each type of asset in the respective column. Please deduct the amount of any indebtedness which you may have.

Type of Asset	Husband's Name	Wife's Name	Joint w/spouse
Real estate			
Cash items (including all types of bank accounts)			
Stocks and bonds (taxable and nontaxable)			
Interests in partnerships and closely held corporations			
Notes and mortgages due to you			
Jewelry, art, automobiles, collections, boats or other tangible property of high value			
Life insurance and annuities (face value less loans)			
Pension plans and IRA accounts			
Miscellaneous other property			
Approximate Totals:	$_____	$_____	$_____

APPENDIX B

THIS IS NOT AN APPLICATION
FOR HOMESTEAD EXEMPTION

DECLARATION OF DOMICILE

To the Clerk of the Circuit Court (County Comptroller) _____ County, Florida.

This is my declaration of domicile in the State of _____ , that I am filing this day in accordance and in conformity with Section 222.17, Florida Statutes.

FOR DOMICILES OF THE STATE OF FLORIDA:

I hereby declare that I reside in and maintain a place of abode at (Street and Number) _____ , (City)_____ , (Zip Code)_____ , in _____ County, Florida, which place of abode I recognize and intend to maintain as my permanent home and, if I maintain another place or places of abode in some other state or states, I hereby declare that my above-described residence and abode in the State of Florida constitutes my predominant and principal home, and I intend to continue it permanently as such. I am, at the time of making this declaration, a bona fide resident of the State of Florida residing at (Street and Number) _____ , (City) _____ , (Zip Code) _____ , in _____ County, Florida. I formerly resided at (City) _____ , _____ County, (State) _____ , and the place or places where I maintain another or other place or places of abode are as follows: (Here list street address, city, county and state of any other place or places of abode.)

Signature _____   Signature _____

Print Name _____   Print Name _____

Sworn to and subscribed before me this _____ day of _____ , A.D. 19____.

_____
Signature and Title of Notarizing or Attesting Official

FOR DOMICILES OF STATES OTHER THAN THE STATE OF FLORIDA:

I hereby declare that my domicile is in the State of _____ and that I intend to permanently continue and maintain my domicile in such state. At the time of making this declaration I am a bona fide resident of the State of _____ . My place of abode within the State of Florida, if any, is as follows: (Here list street address, city, and county of place of abode in Florida.)

(Person making declaration may also include such other and further facts with reference to any acts done or performed by such person which such person desires or intends not to be construed as evidencing any intention to establish his domicile within the State of Florida.)

Print Name _____   Signature _____

Sworn to and subscribed before me this _____ day of _____ , A.D. 19____.

_____
Signature and Title of Notarizing or Attesting Official

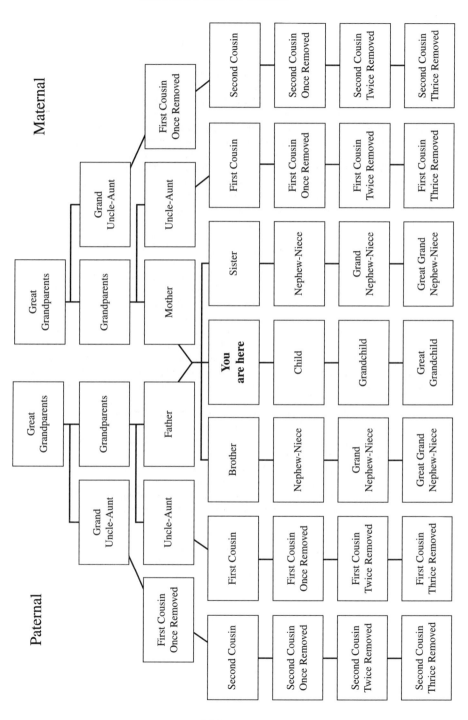

APPENDIX D
DURABLE POWER OF ATTORNEY

KNOW ALL MEN BY THESE PRESENTS, that I, _____, have made, constituted and appointed, and by these presents do make, constitute and appoint _____ as my true and lawful attorney for me and in my name, place and stead:

1. To buy, sell, lease, exchange or otherwise acquire and dispose of all or any part of any real property or tangible or intangible personal property, including stocks, bonds (specifically including United States government bonds which may be redeemed at par in the payment of Federal estate tax), debentures, or other securities, for such price and upon such terms as said attorney may deem proper; to receive or execute, acknowledge and deliver good and sufficient deeds, leases, assignments, stock powers or other instruments for the conveyance or transfer of same with or without covenants or warranties as said attorney may deem proper, and to give or receive good and effective receipts for all or any part of the purchase price, consideration, income or dividends arising therefrom. This authority specifically includes the authority to execute stock powers or similar documents on behalf of the principal and delegate to a transfer agent or similar person the authority to register any stocks, bonds, or other securities either into or out of the principal or nominee's name. This authority further specifically includes the authority to convey or mortgage homestead property. If the principal is married, the attorney in fact may not mortgage or convey homestead property without joinder of the spouse of the principal or the spouse's legal guardian. Joinder by a spouse may be accomplished by the exercise of authority in a durable power of attorney executed by the joining spouse, and either spouse may appoint the other as his attorney in fact.

2. To borrow or loan any sum or sums of money on such terms and conditions and with such security (either real or personal) as said attorney may deem proper, and for that purpose to receive or execute, acknowledge and deliver all promissory notes, bonds, mortgages, security instruments and other instruments or property which said attorney may deem necessary or proper.

3. To deposit money in and withdraw money from any bank, savings and loan association or savings bank (including any account in which I am a joint tenant, tenant by the entirety or the owner-trustee of a Totten trust for another); to execute or endorse checks (including any government checks), withdrawal requests, notes, bonds, drafts or other negotiable or non-negotiable instruments and stock certificates; and to have full access to all safe deposit boxes (including any safe deposit box held jointly with any other person).

4. To ask, demand, compromise, recover and receive all and any sums of money, debts, chattels and effects due or payable or which may at any time be due or payable and upon receipt thereof to make, execute, acknowledge and deliver such receipts, releases, partial releases, satisfactions and other discharges as said attorney may deem necessary or proper.

5. To commence, prosecute, discontinue, compromise or defend all actions or other proceedings in any court or before any commission, board or administrative body.

6. To prepare, execute and file any tax returns required by any municipal, state or federal government or agency thereof and to pay any amount due thereon and to make claim for and collect any refund or rebate on any tax return.

7. To transfer assets to a trust described in Section 733.707(3), Florida Statutes, of which I am the grantor. The said attorney shall not have authority to exercise any general or special power of appointment held by me, to revoke or amend any will or trust agreement (other than a Totten trust) made by me, or to change the ownership or beneficiary designation of any of my life insurance, pension plans, deferred compensation arrangements, or Individual Retirement Accounts.

8. For all or any of the purposes of these presents and for any other purpose, said attorney shall have full power and authority to enter and sign, seal, execute, acknowledge and deliver any contracts, deeds, assignments, satisfactions, releases, partial releases, agreements, stock powers, proxies, motor vehicle title certificates, or other instruments whatsoever, and to draw, accept, make, endorse, discount or otherwise deal with any bills of exchange, checks, promissory notes or other commercial or mercantile instruments.

9. In general to do all other acts, deeds, matters and things whatsoever in or about the undersigned's estate, property and affairs, or to concur with any persons jointly interested therein in doing all acts, deeds,

matters and things herein, either particularly or generally described and any and all other acts, deeds, matters and things though not particularly or generally set forth herein, as fully and effectively to all intents and purposes as the undersigned could do if personally present; and to employ, retain in employment and discharge such persons (both professional and otherwise) as said attorney may deem necessary to assist in the performance of any of the foregoing.

10. If more than one attorney in fact is named above, each of the above named attorneys in fact shall have each and every of the foregoing powers, and it is not necessary for said attorneys to act jointly.

With full power of revocation reserved in the undersigned, but granting to said attorney each and every foregoing power and authority, hereby ratifying and confirming all that said attorney shall lawfully do or cause to be done by virtue hereof; and it is hereby declared that everything said attorney shall do or cause to be done under the provisions hereof after revocation of this power of attorney shall be valid and effectual in favor of any person claiming the benefit thereof who relied upon these presents and had no knowledge or notice of such revocation.

This durable power of attorney shall not be affected by disability of the principal except as provided by statute. It is the intent of the undersigned principal that the power conferred upon the attorney in fact shall be exercisable from the date of this instrument notwithstanding a later disability or incapacity of the principal unless otherwise provided by statute. This durable power of attorney is made in conformance with the provisions of Section 709.08, Florida Statutes.

IN WITNESS WHEREOF, I have hereunto set my hand and seal this _____ day of _____, 199___.

Signed and sealed in the presence of:

_____
Signature of Witness

_____
Print Name of Witness

_____
Signature of Witness

_____
Print Name of Witness

STATE OF FLORIDA
COUNTY OF SARASOTA

The foregoing instrument was acknowledged before me this _____ day of _____, 199___, by _____, who is personally known to me.

_____
Signature of Notary Public

_____
Print Name of Notary Public
Notary Public of State of Florida and my
commission expires on:_____

(NOTARY SEAL)

HEALTH CARE ADVANCE DIRECTIVE

of

(Name)

This document is intended to designate a health care surrogate to direct the course of my medical treatment upon my incapacity to do so, as allowed by Chapter 765, Florida Statutes. It is also intended to express my wishes that life-prolonging procedures be withheld or withdrawn, as allowed by Chapter 765, Florida Statutes. It is also intended to serve as a durable power of attorney for medical care as allowed by Section 709.08, Florida Statutes.

I designate my _____, _____, as my health care surrogate and as my attorney in fact, referred to in this document as my Health Care Agent. If my _____ is unwilling or unable to serve as my Health Care Agent, I designate my _____, _____, as my alternate Health Care Agent.

[* OR alternative second paragraph]

[I designate my children, _____ and _____, to serve jointly as my health care surrogate and as my attorney in fact, referred to in this document as my Health Care Agent. In the event either of my children shall be unable or unwilling to serve or to continue to serve as my health care surrogate, then the other shall serve as my sole alternate health care surrogate. A certificate signed by my alternate health care surrogate and acknowledged before a Notary Public shall be conclusive of the facts stated therein relating to the terms of this instrument, the incapacity or inability to serve of either of my health care surrogates, and the identity of my alternate health care surrogate.]

My Health Care Agent is given complete authority to make all health care decisions for me and to provide informed consent for medical treatment in the event that I am incapacitated to make such decisions or to provide informed consent. Without limiting this broad power of authority, my Health Care Agent is hereby given the specific power and authority to do each of the following:

1. Consult with appropriate health care providers to make health care decisions for me which my Health Care Agent believes I would have made for myself under the circumstances.

2. Arrange for and consent to medical, therapeutic, diagnostic and surgical procedures for me, including the administration of drugs and medications.

3. Enter into and sign, seal, execute, acknowledge and deliver any medical authorizations and consents, contracts, releases, partial releases, agreements or other documents or instruments required in order to carry out my intent.

4. Have access to my clinical records and have authority to authorize the release of information and clinical records to appropriate persons to ensure the continuity of my health care and to process any claims for benefits or insurance payments.

5. Apply for insurance or third party payor benefits, and to apply for public benefits such as Medicare and Medicaid, for me and have access to information regarding my coverage, income and assets to the extent required to make such application.

6. Authorize my transfer and admission to or discharge from any hospital, hospice, nursing home, assisted care facility or other health care facility.

7. Move me from any state to another if my Health Care Agent considers that such move shall be in my best interest.

8. Carry out or authorize others to carry out the directions of the following Living Will Declaration: I willfully and voluntarily make known my desire that my dying shall not be artificially prolonged under the circumstances set forth below.

If at any time I have a terminal condition and if my attending or treating physician and another consulting physician have determined that there is no medical probability of my recovery from such condition, I direct that life-prolonging procedures be withheld or withdrawn when the application of such procedures would serve only to prolong artificially the process of dying, and that I be permitted to die naturally with only the administration of medication or the performance of any medical procedure deemed necessary to provide me with comfort care or to alleviate pain.

Language in the following paragraph can be included or omitted to reflect your wishes:
I do desire that nutrition and hydration (food and water) be withheld or withdrawn when the application of such procedures would serve only to prolong artificially the process of dying. I do accordingly specifically direct that no artificial methods of providing nutrition and hydration (including but not limited to nasogastric tubes) be used if such procedure would serve only to prolong artificially the process of dying.

In the absence of my ability to give directions regarding the use of such life-prolonging procedures, it is my intention that this declaration shall be honored by my family and physician and any others authorized to make treatment decisions on my behalf as the final expression of my legal right to refuse medical or surgical treatment and I accept the consequences for such refusal.

I understand the full import of this declaration, and I am emotionally and mentally competent to make this declaration.

My attending physician, any consulting physician and any other health care provider shall provide my Health Care Agent with information sufficient to permit my Health Care Agent to make informed health care decisions for me. My Health Care Agent's right to consultation and cooperation shall be considered equal to that of mine. My Health Care Agent shall specifically be given information related to my health, including (without limitation): the diagnosis, the prognosis, the alternative treatment modalities available, the possible risks versus benefits of treatment, the side effects of medication, the financial impact of proposed treatment, and the likely outcome of a refusal to consent.

The laws of Florida provide that I have the fundamental right of self-determination regarding decisions pertaining to my own health, including the right to choose or refuse medical treatment. To ensure that this right is not lost or diminished by virtue of later physical or mental incapacity, the law allows me to plan for incapacity by designating another person to direct the course of my medical treatment upon my incapacity. My Health Care Agent is designated as this person, and it is my desire that my Health Care Agent exercise the powers granted herein, even if there are conflicting opinions held by my family, friends, or guardians.

My Health Care Agent shall not be subject to civil or criminal liability for acting as a reasonably prudent person in accordance with the instructions contained in this instrument or for making health care decisions and giving authorizations which my Health Care Agent reasonably believes to be those which I would have made under the existing circumstances.

It is my intent that all power conferred on the Health Care Agent shall be exercisable from the date of this instrument, notwithstanding my later disability or incapacity, unless otherwise provided by statute.

If any part of this instrument shall be invalid, it shall be severed so as to not affect the validity of the remainder of the document. It is my specific direction that the invalidity of the health care surrogate or durable medical power of attorney shall not cause the invalidity of the other.

This instrument shall remain in effect until it is revoked by me. I may revoke this instrument at any time, but I grant every foregoing power, confirming all that my Health Care Agent shall do or cause to be done by virtue hereof. I declare that everything my Health Care Agent shall do or cause to be done under the provisions of this document after revocation of this instrument shall be valid as to any person who relied upon this document and had no knowledge or notice of such revocation.

The powers enumerated in this document are not to be considered as limiting any powers which I may have under the laws of the State of Florida or the United States.

I shall provide an exact copy of this instrument to my Health Care Agent.

IN WITNESS WHEREOF, I have signed this instrument this the _____ day of _____, 199___.

_____

(Name)

WITNESS ATTESTATION

This health care advance directive was signed and sealed by (Name) in our presence.

We certify that both of us are adults and that neither of us is the spouse of (Name), or a blood relative, or an heir to the estate of (Name), or responsible for paying the health care costs of (Name).

_____

Witness   Witness

STATE OF FLORIDA
COUNTY OF SARASOTA

The foregoing instrument was acknowledged before me this ____ day of _____, 199___, by (Name), who is personally known to me or who has produced _____ as identification and who did not take an oath. If no type of identification is indicated, the above-named person is personally known to me.

_____

Signature of Notary Public

_____

Print Name of Notary Public

(NOTARY SEAL)   I am a Notary Public of the State of Florida, and my commission expires on:

_____

APPENDIX F
LIVING WILL DECLARATION

I, (Name), the declarant, willfully and voluntarily make known my desire that my dying shall not be artificially prolonged under the circumstances set forth below, and do hereby declare:

If at any time I have a terminal condition and if my attending or treating physician and another consulting physician have determined that there is no medical probability of my recovery from such condition, I direct that life-prolonging procedures be withheld or withdrawn when the application of such procedures would serve only to prolong artificially the process of dying, and that I be permitted to die naturally with only the administration of medication or the performance of any medical procedure deemed necessary to provide me with comfort care or to alleviate pain.

I <u>do</u> desire that nutrition and hydration (food and water) be withheld or withdrawn when the application of such procedures would serve only to prolong artificially the process of dying. I do accordingly specifically direct that no artificial methods of providing nutrition and hydration (including but not limited to nasogastric tubes) be used if such procedure would serve only to prolong artificially the process of dying.

In the absence of my ability to give directions regarding the use of such life-prolonging procedures, it is my intention that this declaration shall be honored by my family and physician and any others authorized to make treatment decisions on my behalf as the final expression of my legal right to refuse medical or surgical treatment and I accept the consequences for such refusal.

I understand the full import of this declaration, and I am emotionally and mentally competent to make this declaration.

Dated this _____ day of _____, 199___.

_____
(Name)

This declaration was signed by the declarant in the presence of the following two subscribed witnesses, neither of whom is a spouse or blood relative of the declarant. The declarant is known to each of the undersigned and each of the undersigned believes the declarant to be of sound mind.

_____
Witness

_____
Witness

APPENDIX G
FUNDING AND ADMINISTERING YOUR TRUST AGREEMENT

You have participated in the creation of a sophisticated estate plan, whereby your will and trust agreement are designed to operate in conjunction with each other. While people generally understand the operation of their Will, most have questions concerning the new trust agreement. The following summary should answer many of your questions concerning the funding of the trust agreement and its day to day operations.

Transferring Assets to Your Trust

It is most important that most if not all of your assets be transferred to your trust. If assets are not transferred to the trust, then they will not be subject to the terms of the trust agreement until after your death, and you can lose a major benefit of the trust agreement. The number of assets and the type of assets placed in the trust will vary from person to person. Below are some suggestions on transferring the various types of assets.

1. **Stocks and Bonds.** Securities may be transferred through your stockbroker with re-registration so that they are no longer in your individual name, but are registered in your name as the trustee as follows:

"(Name) tte u/a dtd _____, f/b/o (Name) et al."

This means (Name) as trustee under agreement dated _____, for the benefit of (Name), and others.

Generally, your stockbroker or others in his or her office will request to see a copy of your Trust Agreement. They need to know that the Trust Agreement does exist, and they may want to check several of its provisions.

Street Accounts. Frequently, stockbrokers will hold securities for you as trustee in what is known as a "street account" or "street name account" or "nominee account." This means that the stockbrokers' company will hold the securities in its name and then follow your instructions as trustee for the trading of securities. You do not receive physical delivery of the securities; they are simply held by the stockbroker for you.

Bank Custody Accounts. When a corporate fiduciary such as a bank is named as successor trustee, securities and similar assets can often be delivered to the bank trust department to hold in custody following your instructions as the current trustee. Sometimes the securities are placed in the bank nominee's account, which is an account very similar to the broker's street account. The bank, however, will charge a fee for holding the securities and transmitting any dividends or interest to you. This arrangement can be useful to establish a working relationship with the bank's trust department in order to see how they perform with a custody account, before they become your successor trustee.

The bank's trust investment department can be called upon to upgrade the service which the bank is rendering from a custody account to an investment management account. With an investment management account, the trust department gives advice concerning the buying and selling of your securities. Occasionally, the client who is serving as trustee will decide to turn the entire management of the trust over to the trust department and resign as trustee.

Unregistered Securities. Many people have what are known as bearer bonds. Typically, these are municipal bonds and have no individual owner's name on them; they belong to whoever holds them. This type of ownership is fraught with potential problems, since anyone who holds the security is considered to be the owner. This means that the bearer bond has to be treated just as cash.

We recommend that bearer bonds be kept in a Florida safe deposit box (Florida does not seal safe deposit boxes upon the death of an owner), with a note in the following form attached to the bearer bonds:

"For value received, I hereby sell, assign and transfer to (Name) as trustee u/a dated _____, the following described bearer bonds (describe them by name, denomination, due date and interest rate on the bonds).

Dated this ____ day of _____, 199___

Signature_____(Seal)."

We also recommend that the original broker's confirmation slip be either retained with the bond or kept in your separate records. This confirmation slip will also establish who originally purchased the bearer bond. Do not place bearer bonds in a joint box unless the bearer bonds are intended to be made joint, and you discuss this with the attorney who assisted you in the trust. The appropriate notations should then be made with a memorandum attached to the securities stating that they are held as joint tenants with right of survivorship with the named individual.

2. Florida Real Estate. Real estate requires some care to correctly transfer the title of the real estate to your trust. Real estate held in Florida or a note and mortgage to be transferred to the trust should be transferred by a deed or an assignment of mortgage by special instruments drafted by an attorney who practices real estate or trust law. Generally, this transfer will be accomplished by a special type of deed which will incorporate many of the trustee's powers in the deed itself. The same is also true of an assignment of the note and mortgage.

If the real estate is your home and constitutes what is known as your "homestead" for Florida real estate tax purposes, please consult with your attorney about the advisability of transferring this property to your trust.

It may be necessary to show a copy of your trust at the Property Appraiser's Office (tax assessor) so that department may make the appropriate changes in their records. We presently have an informal arrangement with the Property Appraiser's office so that they will accept a statement (on the deed transferring your property to the trustee) that you own not less than a life estate interest in the real estate to be a trust asset. This avoids the inconvenience of your having to go to the Property Appraiser's office and show your Trust Agreement to the clerks in that office.

3. Out of State Real Estate. The conveyance of real estate located outside the State of Florida can present special problems. Each state's laws are different, and the real estate is governed by the law of the state in which the real estate is located. It is important that an attorney who is experienced in both real estate law and trust law in the state where the real estate is located be retained to transfer the real estate to the trust. That attorney should review the Trust Agreement to make sure that the terms of the trust agreement will not be in conflict with that state's laws.

4. Bank Accounts. Checking accounts, savings accounts, certificates of deposit, and similar types of accounts including money markets may be treated very much as securities. The registration may be as follows:

"(Name) as Trustee u/a dated _____, f/b/o (Name) et al."

This title should appear on all of the documents creating the account. Frequently, the financial institution will shorten the title in informal correspondence to just (Name), Trustee. This is perfectly permissible, but the title in the bank's registry of accounts should be in the longer form.

5. Life Insurance. Generally, if you are the owner of the life insurance and you are the insured, it is not necessary to transfer the life insurance to the trust. The primary purpose of many trusts is to avoid having the assets subject to probate, and life insurance on your life payable to an individual is not a probate asset. However, life insurance which you own which insures the life of another, such as a spouse or a child, should be transferred to the trust in most instances. Insurance companies provide forms for transferring life insurance. You may contact your life insurance company for their form to transfer life insurance to your trust.

6. Tax Identification Number. When registering securities, bank accounts or other assets, you may be asked for a tax identification number for the trust. The tax identification number for your trust is your social security number.

Several years ago, trusts such as yours were required to apply for a separate taxpayer identification number. The law has now changed, and it is no longer necessary to use a special tax identification number.

Administering Your Trust

As trustee, you are the person responsible for administering the trust and the trust assets. As the grantor, you have the right to alter or amend the trust any time you choose. You can revoke it, or take the income or take principal if you choose. However, even though the interests which you have as the grantor, beneficiary and as trustee are all inclusive, it is important that certain formalities be observed.

You should keep good records. While you may know what has transpired, the successor trustee may find it very difficult to follow your record keeping system. Assets transferred in the trust, transferred out of the trust, assets which are purchased, sold, and all other transactions involving trust assets should be clearly documented. Your tax basis for the assets transferred to the trust should be determined and recorded. If the assets which are in the trust are substantial and you find the record keeping burdensome, then a professional bookkeeper or an accountant or a bank with a trust department may be utilized to provide the record keeping services.

The same degree of care which you exercised over your assets before they were shifted to your trust should be continued after the assets are transferred to the trust. Stocks, bonds and particularly bearer bonds, should be kept in a safe deposit box and clearly identified as noted above. Insurance should be carried on property in the appropriate amounts.

Trust assets which you hold as trustee may be kept in the joint box or in a box which is in your name alone. However, these assets should be clearly shown and registered to the trustee so that there is no confusion as to the ownership of these assets.

Reporting the Trust for Tax Purposes

Your trust is considered, while you are alive, to be in many respects your alter ego. This is true for federal income tax purposes. In reporting trust income for federal income tax purposes it is only necessary that you report the trust income in the appropriate schedules on your own personal 1040. It is not necessary to file a separate trust income tax return.

The Florida Intangible Tax Return provides for the reporting of intangible assets held by a trustee. This form may be confusing since it says that fiduciaries (trustees) may not take the $20,000 per person per year exclusion. Trusts such as yours do not need to file a separate Florida Intangible Tax Return. You may report all of the securities on your personal Florida Intangible Tax Return and take the $20,000 exclusion which is available to you as an individual. Do not, however, take an additional $20,000 deduction by reason of the trust.

APPENDIX H
ESTATE AND GIFT TAX TABLES

UNIFIED TRANSFER TAX
(POST-1976 TRANSFERS)

Tax on Taxable Amount	Tax First Column	Rate on Excess
-0-	-0-	18%
10,000	1,800	20%
20,000	3,800	22%
40,000	8,200	24%
60,000	13,000	26%
80,000	18,200	28%
100,000	23,800	30%
150,000	38,800	32%
250,000	70,800	34%
500,000	155,800	37%
750,000	248,300	39%
1,000,000	345,800	41%
1,250,000	448,300	43%
1,500,000	555,800	45%
2,000,000	780,800	49%
2,500,000	1,025,800	53%
3,000,000	1,290,800	55%
10,000,000	5,140,800	60%
21,040,000	11,764,800	55%

Note: Always deduct unified credit (see next page)
from tentative tax to get actual tax.

UNIFIED CREDIT

Deaths (or Gifts) in	Amount of Credit	Equivalent Exempt Amount*
1981	47,000	175,625
1982	62,800	225,000
1983	79,300	275,000
1984	96,300	325,000
1985	121,800	400,000
1986	155,800	500,000
1987-1997	192,800	600,000
1998	202,050	625,000
1999	211,300	650,000
2000	220,550	675,000
2001	220,550	675,000
2002	229,800	700,000
2003	229,800	700,000
2004	287,300	850,000
2005	326,300	950,000
2006	345,800	1,000,000

*For gift tax purposes, this assumes no pre-1977 taxable gifts in excess of the $30,000 exemption.

MAXIMUM CREDIT
FOR STATE DEATH TAXES

Taxable Estate	Adjusted Taxable Estate*	Credit On Left Columns	Credit Rate On Excess
100,000	40,000	-0-	0.8%
150,000	90,000	400	1.6%
200,000	140,000	1,200	2.4%
300,000	240,000	3,600	3.2%
500,000	440,000	10,000	4.0%
700,000	640,000	18,000	4.8%
900,000	840,000	27,600	5.6%
1,100,000	1,040,000	38,800	6.4%
1,600,000	1,540,000	70,800	7.2%
2,100,000	2,040,000	106,800	8.0%
2,600,000	2,540,000	146,800	8.8%
3,100,000	3,040,000	190,800	9.6%
3,600,000	3,540,000	238,800	10.4%
4,100,000	4,040,000	290,800	11.2%
5,100,000	5,040,000	402,800	12.0%
6,100,000	6,040,000	522,800	12.8%
7,100,000	7,040,000	650,800	13.6%
8,100,000	8,040,000	786,800	14.4%
9,100,000	9,040,000	930,800	15.2%
10,100,000	10,040,000	1,082,800	16.0%

*"Adjusted taxable estate" means the taxable estate reduced
by $60,000 [IRC 2011(b)].

GIFTS TO MINORS

	Outright Gift	Custodianship	Guardianship	Regular Trust	Sec. 2503(b) Trust	Sec. 2503(c) Trust
Is income for minor generally?	Yes	Yes	Yes	Trust controls	Mandatory distribution	Discretionary distribution
Is use of principal for minor generally?	Yes	Yes	Yes	Trust controls	Trust controls	Discretionary distribution
Judicial supervision	No	No	Yes		No	
Fiduciary qualifications	None	Any adult or trust company	Court-approved	Donor's choice		
Tax risk—donor is fiduciary	No	Yes	No	Possible		
Accounting	No	Records kept; possible accounting	Yes; courts require	Generally, only private records need to be kept		
Investments	Unlimited	Limited	Limited	Generally, as donor authorized in trust		
When does minor get title?	Immediately	Immediately	Immediately	On termination income or earlier principal distribution of trust		
When does minor get possession?	Immediately	Age of majority	Age of majority	Trust controls	Trust controls	Generally, age of majority
When can minor dispose of gift property?	Generally, age of majority	Age of majority	Age of majority	Trust controls	Trust controls	Generally, age of majority

APPENDIX J
MARITAL DEDUCTION
RESIDUARY TRUST SHARE PLAN

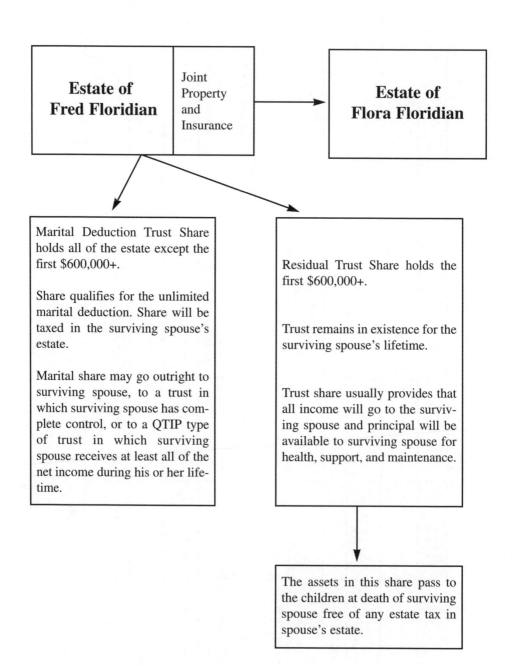

Estate of
Fred Floridian

Joint
Property
and
Insurance

Estate of
Flora Floridian

Marital Deduction Trust Share holds all of the estate except the first $600,000+.

Share qualifies for the unlimited marital deduction. Share will be taxed in the surviving spouse's estate.

Marital share may go outright to surviving spouse, to a trust in which surviving spouse has complete control, or to a QTIP type of trust in which surviving spouse receives at least all of the net income during his or her lifetime.

Residual Trust Share holds the first $600,000+.

Trust remains in existence for the surviving spouse's lifetime.

Trust share usually provides that all income will go to the surviving spouse and principal will be available to surviving spouse for health, support, and maintenance.

The assets in this share pass to the children at death of surviving spouse free of any estate tax in spouse's estate.

APPENDIX K
PRENUPTIAL AGREEMENT

THIS AGREEMENT, made this the _____ day of _____, 199___, by and between _____ hereinafter referred to as "HUSBAND," and _____ hereinafter referred to as "WIFE."

W I T N E S S E T H:

WHEREAS, Husband and Wife contemplate marriage to each other; and,

WHEREAS, Husband and Wife each have children by a previous marriage and it is their intention that each will obtain no rights of any kind or character in the estate of the other solely by reason of their marriage; and,

WHEREAS, Husband has fully informed Wife of his financial condition and the nature and extent of his property, a list of his approximate assets being attached hereto as Exhibit A, and Wife has fully informed Husband of her financial condition and the nature and extent of her property, a list of her approximate assets being attached hereto as Exhibit B, and each has otherwise made a fair disclosure to the other of his or her estate.

NOW THEREFORE, in consideration of the premises, and in consideration of the promise to marry and the marriage, the parties do hereby agree as follows:

1. Each party does waive and relinquish all of his or her rights in and to the real, personal and mixed property owned by the other party, either now or acquired in the future, including but not limited to dower, curtesy, homestead, exempt property, elective share, right or preference to serve as a personal representative of the deceased spouse's estate or as a guardian of the other, and all other statutory rights, and all rights as a widow, widower or heir of the other party under the laws of any State that are now in force or which may be in force in the future, and all other interests, rights, property, claims, demands and titles at law or in equity which either party does or may have in the other party's property. By this agreement, each party relinquishes, quitclaims and grants to the other party, his or her heirs and assigns forever, all of the above-mentioned interests in the other party's property (including any interest in any pension or profit sharing plan, IRA or other retirement property) so that each party, his or her heirs, personal representatives and assigns shall have no right, title or claim to any of these interests except to the extent the other party may have made specific provisions as hereinafter provided in Paragraph 3. Each party agrees to consent to any election made by the other party in connection with any pension or profit sharing plan, IRA or other retirement plan owned by the other party and the parties also agree that the surviving party will disclaim any right to any interest in any pension or profit sharing plan, IRA or other retirement plan owned by the first decedent

unless the first decedent has specifically named the surviving party as a beneficiary as hereinafter provided in Paragraph 3. Each party further agrees that he or she will make no further claims upon the other party's estate, heirs, personal representatives and assigns after the death of the other party or of any interest in any real, personal or mixed property of which the other party may die seized and possessed except as hereinafter provided in Paragraph 3.

2. The parties agree that each shall manage, control, sell, mortgage, convey and transfer their separate property during the marriage and each party agrees in the future to execute, or join as a party, in any instrument when requested to do so by the other party, in order to divest him or her of any claim, title or interest in the property of the other party.

3. Nothing in this agreement shall be construed to prohibit either party from providing for the other party by the terms and provisions of his or her Last Will and Testament, nor shall this agreement be construed to restrict the surviving party from claiming property subsequently given by one party to the other party or owned by the parties as joint tenants with right of survivorship or as tenants by the entireties, or as a beneficiary of any trust instrument, including a Totten Trust, or as a designated beneficiary of any life insurance, annuity, retirement plan or benefit.

4. The parties agree that each shall be responsible for his or her necessities and neither party shall be responsible or liable for necessities of the other party or liable to creditors of the other party for necessities furnished the other party, including but not limited to expenses incurred for the health, maintenance and support of the other party; provided, however, this shall not be construed to prohibit the parties from commingling assets to provide for their combined living expenses, if both parties desire to do so.

5. In the event of a dissolution of marriage of the parties, this agreement shall be of full force and effect and each party agrees that he or she shall have no claim against the other party's property for alimony, support or property settlements. Any property owned jointly by the parties shall be divided in a ratio of each of the respective party's consideration contributed to the said joint property.

6. The parties declare that they have read this agreement carefully, have disclosed the extent, nature and value of their property each to the other, and have discussed the effect of this agreement. Husband has received independent legal counsel and advice from his attorney, _____, and Wife has received independent legal counsel and advice from her attorney, _____.

7. It is agreed that the law of the State of Florida shall be applicable to this agreement and that this agreement shall be binding upon the parties hereto, their heirs, legatees, devisees, personal representatives, Trustees and assigns.

8. This agreement cannot be amended or revoked except by a written instrument signed by both parties in the presence of two witnesses and acknowledged by the parties before a Notary Public.

IN WITNESS WHEREOF, the parties have hereunto set their hands and seals to this agreement on the date first above written.

Signed and sealed in the
    presence of:

_____(SEAL)

                                                          HUSBAND

_____

As to Husband

_____(SEAL)

                                                          WIFE

_____

As to Wife

STATE OF _____
COUNTY OF _____

The foregoing instrument was acknowledged before me this _____ day of _____, 199___, by _____ and _____, who are personally known to me or who have produced _____ as identification and who did not take an oath. If no type of identification is indicated, the above-named persons are personally known to me.

_____

Signature of Notary Public

_____

Print Name of Notary Public

(NOTARY SEAL)

I am a Notary Public of the
State of _____
and my commission expires on

_____

APPENDIX L
PROBATE FORMS

IN THE CIRCUIT COURT FOR _____ COUNTY, FLORIDA
IN RE: ESTATE OF   PROBATE DIVISION

                                             File Number _____

                                             Division _____

Deceased.

PETITION FOR ADMINISTRATION
(testate Florida resident — single petitioner)

Petitioner, _____ alleges:

   1. Petitioner has an interest in the above estate as _____
_____

Petitioner's address is _____
_____

and the name and office address of petitioner's attorney are set forth at the end of this petition.

   2. Decedent, _____
whose last known address was_____
and, if known, whose age was _____ and whose social security number is _____
died on , _____19 _____at_____
and on the date of death decedent was domiciled in _____County, Florida

3. So far as is known, the names of the beneficiaries of this estate and of the decedent's surviving spouse, if any, their addresses and relationship to decedent, and the dates of birth of any who are minors, are:

NAME   ADDRESS   RELATIONSHIP   DATE OF BIRTH (if Minor)

4. Venue of this proceeding is in this county because _____

_____

5. _____

whose address is _____

and who is qualified under the laws of the State of Florida to serve as personal represen-

tative of the decedent's estate is entitled to preference in appointment as personal repre-

sentative because _____

6. The nature and approximate value of the assets in this estate are

7. This estate_____be required to file a federal estate tax return.

8. The original of the decedent's last will, dated _____, 19_____,

_____

is in the possession of the court or accompanies this petition.

9. Petitioner is unaware of any unrevoked will or codicil of decedent other than as

set forth in paragraph 8.

Petitioner requests that the decedent's will be admitted to probate and that _____

_____

be appointed personal representative of the estate of the decedent.

Under penalties of penury, I declare that I have read the foregoing, and the facts

alleged are true, to the best of my knowledge and belief.

Signed on _____, 19_____.

_____

                                        Petitioner

_____

          Attorney for Petitioner

Florida Bar No. _____

_____

_____

          (address)

Telephone: _____

IN THE CIRCUIT COURT FOR _____ COUNTY, FLORIDA

IN RE: ESTATE OF

PROBATE DIVISION

File Number _____

Division _____

Deceased.

ORDER ADMITTING WILL TO PROBATE
AND APPOINTING PERSONAL REPRESENTATIVE
(self-proved)

The instrument presented to this court as the last will of

_____,

deceased, having been executed in conformity with law, and made self-proved at the time of its execution by the acknowledgment of the decedent and the affidavits of the witnesses, each made before an officer authorized to administer oaths and evidenced by the officer's certificate attached to or following the will in the form required by law, and no objection having been made to its probate, and the court finding that the decedent died on _____, 19 _____. It is

ADJUDGED that the will dated _____, 19 _____and attested by

_____

_____

as subscribing and attesting witnesses, is admitted to probate according to law as and for the last will of the decedent, and it is further

ADJUDGED that _____
is appointed personal representative of the estate of the decedent, and that upon taking the prescribed oath, filing designation of resident agent and acceptance, and entering into bond in the sum of _____
letters of administration shall be issued.

ORDERED on _____, 19_____.

_____
Circuit Judge

Bar Form No. P-3.0420
© Florida Lawyers Support Services, Inc.
Renewed August 1993

IN THE CIRCUIT COURT FOR _____ COUNTY, FLORIDA

IN RE: ESTATE OF

PROBATE DIVISION
File Number _____
Division _____

Deceased.

OATH OF PERSONAL REPRESENTATIVE
DESIGNATION OF RESIDENT AGENT, AND ACCEPTANCE

STATE OF FLORIDA
COUNTY OF _____

I, _____(Affiant)
state under oath that:

1. I have been appointed personal representative of the estate of _____
_____, deceased.
2. I will faithfully administer the estate of the decedent according to law.
3. My place of residence is _____

and my post office address is _____
_____.

4. I hereby designate _____
who (is)(is not) a member of The Florida Bar, a resident of _____County, Florida
whose place of residence is _____
and whose post office address is _____
as my agent for the service of process or notice in any action against me, either in my representative capacity, or personally, if the personal action accrued in the administration of
the estate.

_____
Affiant

Sworn to and subscribed to before me on _____, 19 ____ by Affiant, who is personally known to me _____ or who produced _____ as identification.
　　　　　　　　　　　(yes or no)　　　　　　　　(type of identification)

_____
Notary Public State of Florida
My Commission Expires:
My Commission Number is:
(Affix Notarial Seal)

ACCEPTANCE
I CERTIFY that I am a permanent resident of _____County, Florida, residing at
the place indicated above. I hereby accept the foregoing designation as Resident Agent.
Signed on _____, 19 _____.

_____
Resident Agent

[Print or Type Names Under All Signatures Lines]

Bar Form No. P-3.0600
©Florida Lawyers Support Services, Inc.
Revised October 1, 1995

221

IN THE CIRCUIT COURT FOR _____ COUNTY, FLORIDA

IN RE: ESTATE OF

PROBATE DIVISION

File Number _____

Division _____

Deceased.

LETTERS OF ADMINISTRATION
(single personal representative)

TO ALL WHOM IT MAY CONCERN

WHEREAS, _____
a resident of _____
died on _____, 19 _____, owning assets in the State of Florida and

WHEREAS, _____
has been appointed personal representative of the estate of the decedent and has performed
all acts prerequisite to issuance of Letters of Administration in the estate,

NOW, THEREFORE, I, the undersigned circuit judge, declare _____
_____
duly qualified under the laws of the State of Florida to act as personal representative of
the estate of _____
deceased, with full power to administer the estate according to law; to ask, demand, sue
for, recover and receive the property of the decedent; to pay the debts of the decedent as
far as the assets of the estate will permit and the law directs; and to make distribution of
the estate according to law.

ORDERED on _____, 19_____.

_____
Circuit Judge

IN THE CIRCUIT COURT FOR _____ COUNTY, FLORIDA

IN RE: ESTATE OF

PROBATE DIVISION

File Number_____

Division _____

Deceased.

NOTICE OF ADMINISTRATION

The administration of the estate of _____

deceased, File Number _____, is pending in the Circuit Court for _____

County, Florida, Probate Division, the address of which is _____

_____

The names and addresses of the personal representative and the personal representative's attorney are set forth below.

ALL INTERESTED PERSONS ARE NOTIFIED THAT:

All persons on whom this notice is served who have objections that challenge the validity of the will, the qualifications of the personal representative, venue, or jurisdiction of this Court are required to file their objections with this Court WITHIN THE LATER OF THREE MONTHS AFTER THE DATE OF THE FIRST PUBLICATION OF THIS NOTICE OR THIRTY DAYS AFTER THE DATE OF SERVICE OF A COPY OF THIS NOTICE ON THEM.

All creditors of the decedent and other persons having claims or demands against decedent's estate on whom a copy of this notice is served within three months after the date of the first publication of this notice must file their claims with this Court WITHIN THE LATER OF THREE MONTHS AFTER THE DATE OF THE FIRST PUBLICATION OF THIS NOTICE OR THIRTY DAYS AFTER THE DATE OF SERVICE OF A COPY OF THIS NOTICE ON THEM.

All other creditors of the decedent and persons having claims or demands against the decedent's estate must file their claims with this court WITHIN THREE MONTHS AFTER THE DATE OF THE FIRST PUBLICATION OF THIS NOTICE.

ALL CLAIMS, DEMANDS AND OBJECTIONS NOT SO FILED WILL BE FOREVER BARRED.

The date of the first publication of this Notice is _____

Attorney for Personal Representative:

Personal Representative:

_____

_____

Attorney

Name

Florida Bar No. _____

_____

_____

_____

_____

(address)

(address)

Telephone: _____

Bar Form No. P-3.0800
©Florida Lawyers Support Services, Inc.
Revised August 1993

IN THE CIRCUIT COURT FOR _____ COUNTY, FLORIDA

IN RE: ESTATE OF

PROBATE DIVISION

File Number _____

Division _____

Deceased.

PROOF OF SERVICE OF NOTICE OF ADMINISTRATION

I CERTIFY that on _____, 19 _____, a copy of the attached Notice of Administration was mailed by United States registered or certified mail, return receipt requested, postage prepaid, or was delivered in a manner permitted by Fla.Prob.R. 5.040, to:

Signed receipts or other evidence that delivery was made to, or refused by, each addressee or the addressee's agent are attached.

Under penalties of perjury, I declare that I have read the foregoing, and the facts alleged are true, to the best of my knowledge and belief.

Signed on _____, 19 _____.

_____
Attorney

Florida Bar No. _____

_____

_____
(address)

Telephone: _____

[Print or Type Names Under All Signature Lines]

IN THE CIRCUIT COURT FOR _____ COUNTY, FLORIDA

IN RE: ESTATE OF

PROBATE DIVISION

File Number_____

Division _____

Deceased.

STATEMENT REGARDING CREDITORS
(individual)

The undersigned, _____
as the personal representative of the estate of _____,
deceased, alleges:

1. A Notice of Administration in the estate of the decedent has been published as required by law, with the first publication occurring on _____. 19_____.

2. Diligent search has been made to ascertain the names and location or mailing addresses of all creditors of the decedent and of all other persons having claims or demands against the estate.

3. The names and, if known, the addresses of all creditors and other persons ascertained to have claims or demands against the estate and who have not filed a timely claim, or who have not had their claim included in a Personal Representatives Proof of Claim filed in this proceeding, are:

    None

[Strike out inapplicable statement]

    Set forth on a schedule attached hereto.

4. A copy of the Notice of Administration was served on each of the persons named on the attached schedule (if any) within three months after the first publication of the Notice of Administration except as otherwise indicated on that schedule.

Under penalties of perjury, I declare that I have read the foregoing, and the facts alleged are true, to the best of my knowledge and belief.

Signed on _____, 19 _____.

_____
Attorney for Personal Representative

_____
Personal Representative

Florida Bar No._____

_____

_____
(address)

Telephone:_____

IN THE CIRCUIT COURT FOR _____ COUNTY, FLORIDA

IN RE: ESTATE OF

PROBATE DIVISION

File Number _____

Division _____

Deceased.

INVENTORY

The undersigned personal representative of the estate of _____ _____, deceased, submits this inventory of all the property of the estate that has come into the hands, possession, control, or knowledge of this personal representative:

REAL ESTATE IN FLORIDA — Exempt Homestead:

Description

REAL ESTATE IN FLORIDA — Non-Exempt Homestead:

Description   Estimated Fair Market Value

(Whether homestead property is exempt from the claims of creditors, whether it is properly devised and whether it is a probate asset may have to be determined by appropriate proceedings.)

Bar Form No. P-3.0900-1 of 3
©Florida Lawyers Support Services, Inc.
Revised October 1, 1996

OTHER REAL ESTATE IN FLORIDA:

Description   Estimated Fair Market Value

Total Real Estate in Florida — Except Exempt Homestead $ _____

PERSONAL PROPERTY WHEREVER LOCATED:

Description   Estimated Fair Market Value

Total Personal Property — Wherever Located $ _____

TOTAL OF ALL PERSONAL PROPERTY AND FLORIDA REAL ESTATE

(Except exempt homestead) $ _____

All real estate located outside the State of Florida owned by the decedent of which the personal representative is aware, if any, is described on a schedule attached hereto. [If none, so indicate]

NOTICE: Each beneficiary has the right to request a written explanation of how the inventory value of any asset was determined, including whether the personal representative obtained an independent appraisal for that asset and from whom the appraisal was obtained.

Under penalties of perjury, I declare that I have read the foregoing, and the facts alleged are true to the best of my knowledge and belief.

Signed on _____, 19 _____.

_____   _____
Attorney for Personal Representative   Personal Representative

Florida Bar No. _____

_____

_____
(address)

Telephone: _____   [Print or Type Names Under All Signature Lines]

IN THE CIRCUIT COURT FOR _____ COUNTY, FLORIDA

IN RE: ESTATE OF

PROBATE DIVISION

File Number _____

Division _____

Deceased.

PERSONAL REPRESENTATIVE'S PROOF OF CLAIM

The undersigned, as personal representative of the above estate, alleges:

1. This personal representative has paid the following debts of the decedent:

Name of Creditor	Explanation	Amount

2. This personal representative intends to pay the following debts of the decedent:

Name of Creditor	Explanation	Amount

Under penalties of perjury, I declare that I have read the foregoing, and the facts alleged are true, to the best of my knowledge and belief.

Signed on _____, 19 _____.

_____

_____
Attorney for Personal Representative

Florida Bar No. _____

_____

_____
(address)

Telephone: _____

Bar Form No. P-3.1000
©Florida Lawyers Support Services, Inc.
Reviewed August 1993

IN THE CIRCUIT COURT FOR _____ COUNTY, FLORIDA

IN RE: ESTATE OF

Deceased.

PROBATE DIVISION

File Number _____

Division _____

PETITION FOR DISCHARGE
(single personal representative)

Petitioner, _____
as personal representative of the above estate, alleges:

1. The decedent, _____
a resident of _____, died on _____, 19____,
and Letters of Administration were issued to petitioner on _____ 19 __.

2. Petitioner files herewith either a Final Accounting containing a complete report of all cash and property transactions and of all receipts and disbursements since the commencement of administration of this estate, or since the date of the last accounting filed herein, if any, or waivers signed by all interested persons, other than petitioner, waiving the filing of a final accounting.

3. Petitioner has fully administered this estate by making payment, settlement, or other disposition of all claims and debts that were presented, and by paying or making provision for the payment of all taxes and expenses of administration.

4. Petitioner has filed all required estate tax returns with the Internal Revenue Service and with the Department of Revenue of the State of Florida, and has obtained and filed with this court evidence of the satisfaction of this estate's obligations for both federal and Florida estate taxes, if any.

5. The amount of compensation paid or to be paid to the personal representative, attorneys, accountants, appraisers, or other agents employed by the personal representative is set forth in Exhibit A attached hereto.

6. Petitioner has made or proposes to make distribution of the assets of this estate as reflected in the plan of distribution set forth in the schedule attached hereto as Exhibit B.

7. The only persons, other than petitioner, having an interest in this proceeding and their respective addresses are:

8. Any objections to the Petition for Discharge, the Final Accounting, the compensation paid or proposed to be paid, or the proposed distribution of assets, must be filed and served within 30 days from the date of service of the last of the Petition for Discharge or Final Accounting. Within 90 days after filing of the objection, a notice of hearing thereon must be served, or the objection is abandoned.

9. Objections, if any, shall be in writing and shall state with particularity the item or items to which the objection is directed and the grounds on which the objection is based.

Petitioner requests that, after satisfactory proof has been presented that distribution has been made in accordance with the schedule of distribution and that claims of creditors have been paid or otherwise disposed of, an order be entered discharging petitioner as personal representative of this estate and releasing the surety on any bond which petitioner may have posted in this proceeding from any further liability on it.

Under penalties of perjury, I declare that I have read the foregoing, and the facts alleged are true, to the best of my knowledge and belief

Signed on _____, 19 _____.

_____

Petitioner

_____

Attorney for Personal Representative

Florida Bar No. _____

_____

_____

(address)

Telephone: _____

[Print or Type Names Under All Signature Lines]

IN THE CIRCUIT COURT FOR _____ COUNTY, FLORIDA

IN RE: ESTATE OF

PROBATE DIVISION

File Number _____

Division _____

Deceased.

WAIVER OF ACCOUNTING AND PORTIONS OF PETITION FOR DISCHARGE; WAIVER OF SERVICE OF PETITION FOR DISCHARGE; AND RECEIPT OF BENEFICIARY AND CONSENT TO DISCHARGE

The undersigned _____,
whose address is _____
_____

and whose social security or tax identification number is _____
and who has an interest in the above estate as _____, hereby:

(a) Expressly acknowledges that the undersigned is aware of the right to have a final accounting,

(b) Waives the filing and service of a final or other accounting by the personal representative;

(c) Waives the inclusion in the Petition for Discharge of the amount of compensation paid or to be paid to the personal representative(s), attorneys, accountants, appraisers, or other agents employed by the personal representative(s), and the manner of determining the compensation;

(d) Expressly acknowledges that the undersigned has actual knowledge of the amount and manner of determining the compensation of the personal representative(s), attorneys, accountants, appraisers, or other agents; has agreed to the amount and manner of determining such compensation; and waives any objections to the payment of such compensation;

(e) Waives the inclusion in the Petition for Discharge of a plan of distribution;

(f) Waives service of the Petition for Discharge of the personal representative and all notice thereof upon the undersigned;

(g) Acknowledges receipt of complete distribution of the share of the estate to which the undersigned was entitled; and

(h) Consents to the entry of an order discharging the personal representative without notice, hearing or waiting period and without further accounting.

Signed on _____, 19 _____.

_____
Beneficiary
[Print or Type Names Under All Signature Lines]

Bar Form No. P-5.0570
©Florida Lawyers Support Services, Inc.
Revised October 1,1996

232

IN THE CIRCUIT COURT FOR _____ COUNTY, FLORIDA

IN RE: ESTATE OF

PROBATE DIVISION

File Number _____

Division _____

Deceased.

ORDER OF DISCHARGE
(single personal representative)

On the Petition for Discharge of _____
as personal representative of the estate of _____,
deceased, the court finding that the estate has been fully administered and properly distributed, that claims of creditors have been paid or otherwise disposed of, that the tax
imposed by Chapter 198 of the Florida Statutes, if any, has been paid, and that the personal representative should be discharged, it therefore is

ADJUDGED that the personal representative is discharged, and the surety on the personal representative's bond, if any, is released from further liability.

ORDERED on _____, 19 _____.

_____
Circuit Judge

Bar Form No. P-5.0800
©Florida Lawyers Support Services, Inc.
Revised October 1, 1996

INDEX

236